I'm Done…
You're Not!

John Hitchcock

John Hitchcock

Contents

John Hitchcock

Prologue

DISCLAIMER:

Teachers can't be put in a single category. They're good, they're bad. Easy job. Summers off. Short days. Take work home or leave it at school.

Being a teacher in the cultural climate today is more difficult than ever. Different social and political groups promote ideas ranging from the coherent to the absurd.

The absurdities simply means you must be intentional in being the teacher you envision.

All these different factions can create in you a sense of frustration and meaningless in your role as a teacher. You just want to help kids become better in their normal lives.

Being intentional at enjoyable activities can require courage, courage you may never realized you possessed. But being intentional being yourself can be rewarding to you and beneficial to others.

FULL DISCLOSURE

In full disclosure, I've had a difficult time writing this book. Here's the thing. It's going to be about my career in teaching, so I don't want to be presumptuous in sharing or self-aggrandizing in stating publicly what I've done. Nor do I want it to be trivial or without meaning.

In retrospect, some of the events are a bit embarrassing. I will share them no matter what and tell myself how to handle things that make me uncomfortable. I told my students the same thing.

"Deal with it!"

My desire is that my stories can give you ideas on how to make your time in teaching fun and effective, even with all the radical changes occurring.

Since we are not identical twins, yours' can't be identical, put perhaps the principles involved could be used to help guide your teaching career.

Most of all, I genuinely hope you can see the unbridled fun I've experienced in fifty-six plus years of teaching.

Doing research (meaning a Google search) on the phrase, "How My Teaching Career was so Much Fun!" revealed that the great majority of blogs or articles were focused on the main philosophical tenants of teaching; "I want to inspire, encourage, motivate, even enthuse my students to be successful…" whatever that means.

You see, I was never smart enough or dedicated enough to wake up in the morning and say, "I'm going to go to school today and inspire my students to be a success."

The closest I can come to being the ideal teacher other folks portray is to awaken with the thoughts of going to school and doing a project or a lesson we (the class and I) could do and have fun with and learn from… ideally both.

So having made my confession, let's get on with seeing what laid the foundation to my becoming, and staying, a teacher.

But First…

Five people could observe the same work of art. There could be five different interpretations or emotional reactions.

The same is true of reading this book. Maybe one story affects you positively, another you may think ridiculous.

Personally, I'm really bothered when I read a very good story or accounting and then the author gives a "moral of the story" which differs radically from mine.

I tell my students, "You are way more adult than you are kid. Your parents don't know it yet, but it's true."

I will do the same with you, the reader.

John Hitchcock

Chap. 1: Preparation for Life

"The events in our lives happen in a sequence in time, but in their significance to ourselves they find their own order the continuous thread of revelation." — Eudora Welty

A First-Grade Thief

The white, one-room school I attended for the first six grades was just over the typical farm fence from our first home. I loved it and learned exciting things as the older students would go to the front and "recite their lessons."

There was a big problem coming, however.

I was absolutely intrigued by chalk and how it felt when writing on the blackboard.

The thrill of writing with chalk overcame a first-grader's sense of morality and I "borrowed" small pieces of chalk most of the times I got to recite and write.

Slipping a piece into my pocket, taking it home and placing it in the desk drawer near my bed, I thought it was hidden securely from my mother.

I would take the chalk outdoors and find any flat surface that was remotely hidden and would show chalk-writing... and I would draw with the chalk.

Eventually my mother opened the drawer with the stash of pilfered chalk.

"John, what's all this chalk in your desk?" Mom's question was more command than question.

"Uhh…I…uh.., took it from school on… accident." I quietly muttered.

Never one to allow an untrue response, my mother said sternly, "You STOLE it, didn't you? Take you book bag. Put the chalk in and we're going to see Miss Twiss right now."

Teachers in those time were also the after-school janitor and maintenance worker, so I knew she was still at school.

The memory is still vivid in my mind as Mom made me say "stole the chalk" rather than "took the chalk."

After being told she could determine the punishment for the crime, Miss Twiss made a remarkably wise decision.

"John, you knew it was wrong. You need to pay for your actions. You will stay after school every day for one week and clean the entire board."

I knew the work involved in the process because I watched her do it at lunch for the afternoon session.

But suddenly the mood of my spirit lightened.

Her voice grew understanding as she said, "However, if you want to, you may write for as long as desired on the board before cleaning it."

For years after that event, I had that thrill of writing new things on blackboards. While white boards and smart boards are good, nothing can surpass the whiteness of chalk on a freshly cleaned board!

My grandmother's attic.

After my grandfather died, my parents, both sisters and I moved into the other end of my grandparents' large, eleven-room farmhouse.

This old house was filled with intriguing treasures and places to explore, but by far the most interesting to me was the attic.

It was large, extending the length of the two-story house, spookily illuminated with diamond shaped windows on each end yet filled with so many treasures to be explored by a twelve-year-old boy. From the 25-35 rifle my father had used as a kid to my grandfather's tools, there was treasure after treasure to explore.

The most exciting of all, however, was a pile of Readers' Digests placed right on the edge of the stairs leading to the attic. They were in that exact location so my grandmother could simply go near the head of the stairs and place the most recently read issue on top.

After getting permission from my grandmother, I reversed the pile, ending with the first issue now on top and the most recent on the bottom. It was exciting to see the oldest was dated October, 1939!

It took me till I was a senior in high school, but reading (ok, skimming lots of the articles) from top to bottom was a real adventure in learning history as seen from different points of view.

I never gave it a thought at the time, but in retrospect, I believe this discovery was one of the fundamental events of life that gave me a tendency to teaching.

Learning became real and fun!

Mr. Baroudi's Drugstore

During eighth-grade, my mother and I stopped by Baroudi's Drugstore for some medication. While there, I noticed an array of interesting looking equipment behind the counter. The excitement level of Mr. Baroudi's voice rose as he explained this was his amateur radio equipment. Thus, explaining the huge antenna dominating the roof of the drugstore.

He offered to show me how it worked, and shortly he was chatting from our location in northern New York with a fellow ham in Georgia. He even allowed me to talk for a minute!

I was hooked, and after attending a ham-radio club meeting with Mr. Baroudi, I ordered my first equipment. Reading through several magazines, I realized to get the best deal I would have to build my own equipment. Further investigation let me to the Heathkit Company, and after raising some chickens, selling eggs and finally the chickens, I had enough money to order a receiver kit, the AR-3 model.

When the box came in the mail, I quickly unpacked it and placed all the parts on the dining room table, completely covering the surface with resistors, capacitors, vacuum tubes and other material. When my parents came home from work, the gasp from my mother was audible.

Her words were filled with doubt. "Are you sure you can do this?"

But my father reduced her hesitancy and gave me confidence. "If other people can do it, I'm sure John can, too."

After a couple of weeks of work the receiver was operational and by the middle of ninth grade, I had studied what was needed for the test and learned the Morse Code, the amateur radio station, KN2RUE, was operational and I was using the code to chat with people all over the United States. And even a few from Germany, South America, and Australia.

Once more in looking back on how seemingly unrelated events work together to frame our present, I believe the contact with Mr. Baroudi and my doing amateur radio created the confidence to risk doing difficult projects during my teaching career.

Eleventh Mountain Musings

Eleventh Mountain began at the back edge of our pasture. It wasn't extremely high, only about 3150 ft. but was quite heavily forested with some interesting ledges to climb. All in all, a bit of a challenge to climb.

Today my parents would be considered "endangering the welfare of a child," but in that day they just told us to "be careful, and don't do anything stupid."

Usually climbed with my cousin or another friend, I really savored making the trek alone. I had my own private rock on the summit of the mountain where I could climb onto, light a fire and heat my hot chocolate and toast fig newtons for lunch.

That rock became a refuge from the world.

I would lay there watching the clouds and imagine the different shapes they formed as they crossed the sky. That alone-time became rich in creating ideas and thinking through the "what if..." parts of life.

Bog Meadow Adventures

When the beaver dam was still active, Bog Meadow had a distinct picturesqueness to it. Not great, but its own degree of beauty.

Once the beavers moved upstream to get more food and build a new dam, Bog Meadow became just a field of tall grass with a slow moving creek running through it.

Nevertheless, it was a special place for me.

Only about a two-and-a-half mile hike from the trailhead up the road from our house, it didn't take long to get there.

Once there, life seemed simpler than it even was.

As a fourteen year old, Bog Meadow became a quiet refuge that I owned alone. Even with friends, when we fished, we weren't together, and often I would sit on the bank of the creek and just think.

Imagining what the inside of a beaver house looked like, I would imagine the beaver-family sitting around talking about their day chewing down trees, laughing as they talked about slapping the water with their tails…

Crazy thoughts for some, but not for me.

Bog Meadow was different.

Sometimes with friends. Filled with laughter of fellow fishermen or hunters (cousins and friends) as we survived day-long rain in a pup tent or enjoyed catching our limit of brook trout and frying them over an open fire.

Life was good and we had no care other than the next cast.

Once more, never envisioning I was being prepared for a crazy adventure into teaching, those mountain-top musings and Bog Meadow fish-fries were quietly preparing me for an enjoyable life in the classroom.

I could savor silence or rejoice in activities of friends.

The good, the bad and the very ugly!

In general, my growing up years were very good. I fished, bowled, played golf, skied, did amateur radio. And enjoyed every minute of it.

But an insidious disaster was lurking just below the surface.

I went to a one-room schoolhouse for grades one through six. The time to climb aboard the big yellow bus and go to the Central School came.

The first day going to the big school down in North Creek started ominously. Sitting in homeroom, the kid in front of me turned around and asked, "You're new here, ain't 'cha? Where ya' from?"

"Up in Bakers Mills." Was my answer.

"Can't be yur very smart. Ain't nobody smart from Dogtown!" he said, using the nickname our town had from the days when there were more dogs in town than people.

10

Life was pretty much normal for a bit of time. Then I got glasses because of measles. That was ok, except they remained unbroken for only a month or so. From that time on the masking tape fixing them was obvious for all to see.

Then the body changes were quietly hard to deal with. By my senior year in high school, I was six feet tall, but weighed only 129 pounds.

On top of that, I had taken a header in the bathtub and broke my two front teeth. Temporary plastic caps became broken on the bottom and very quickly got coffee-stained.

Even though I was a natural introvert and comfortable in life, those extraneous events led me to develop a very poor self-image. In reality, I had a full-blown inferiority complex.

I was happy to be accepted to college. It made my parents proud, but I was quietly terrified. Crowds of greater than four made me nervous. I would go to the dining hall one-hour early to get a table with the few people I knew.

The embarrassment of being poor became obvious when my freshman roommate asked, "When is your mother going to send your winter wardrobe?"

My response was simple. "I just roll the sleeves down." was the answer, but really hid my uneasiness of being unable to afford more clothes.

My sense of self-worth was really taking a beating.

Then came the miracle weekend!

I had returned from an afternoon physics lab about three-thirty, time enough for a short nap before dinner. I slept better than normal and didn't awaken until seven-thirty, too late for dinner.

My roommate had gone home for the weekend so wasn't there to wake me up. Trying to write a lab report was futile and I went back to bed, planning to wake up at six AM in time to make breakfast. But ten AM came as I had to admit I'd missed another meal. Getting out of bed I ate an entire package of chocolate marshmallow twists cookies and drank a quart of milk, then went back to bed.

The intent was to wake up in late afternoon in time to go to dinner at five o'clock. It was seven o'clock when I finally woke up from the intended short nap.

Too late for dinner, I got out of bed, sat at my desk looking blankly at a history assignment, I finally stopped trying to study and lay down on the bed.

Well, you can guess what happened.

The going to sleep, planning on awakening for the next meal continued. Unbelievably, it went until the following Monday. Waking up in time for breakfast, I knew enough about depression and mental awareness to know I WAS IN TROUBLE!

I did the only thing I could think of. Dropping to my knees, I prayed, "Lord, I need Your help."

As I stood to my feet, it was like the voice in my head was real.

"Quit being so selfish. Quit worrying what other people think of you." It was like God singled me out and was getting right to the heart of the matter.

Finally standing, the room itself seemed brighter, my heart felt lighter, and my entire view of the world has been optimistic and exciting.

From that moment, my life has changed.

From that awful weekend but marvelous Monday, I believe the internal confidence and energy to become a freely successful teacher started growing within.

Grades, Amazing Professors and Student-Teaching

Interestingly, after that miracle Monday, my grades went down. Not disastrously and their decline concerned me not one bit. The drop in grades was because I immediately became more social, met more friends, went bowling all night, joined the amateur radio club and worked in the college radio station. In other words, began to enjoy the world around me!

The college I attended, Houghton College in Houghton, New York, was a small Christian school with many outstanding professors. Literally patriarchs and matriarchs of the faith and academic excellence. Most of all, however, these men and women of God could deviate from the subject long enough to give us life-changing words of wisdom.

For instance, our Earth Science class was told that this week's lab would be at the top of Houghton Hill. That was logical since we were studying constellations and other heavenly phenomena.

"See you all there around 9:00." The professor told us the time of the lab.

It was perfect except for the temperature of 10^0F. The lack of a moon and far from lights of the town and campus allowed the stars to burst through, each one like a diamond in the sky.

The professor wasn't there yet, and we were all chatting and shivering as we waited for his lecture. We expected him to point out the various constellation and probably some of the history and mythology involved.

In about five minutes we could hear the crunch of his boots on the hard-frozen snow.

The circle we had formed broke, and he entered the center.

Total silence only seemed to make the stars more vivid.

We remained in silence for about a minute, then the professor began.

Raising his arms towards the stars, he started quoting verses from the book of Psalms, each one proclaiming the Glory of God. Even in the cold, his voice pierced the darkness. For ten minutes he continued.

He then stopped, lowered his arms, turned down the hill, and said, "See you in the morning."

Did you know that at ten degrees tears freeze on your cheeks?

That moment forever changed how I look at the sky... and how I thought about teaching.

I learned so much stuff about being alive from those professors! Even learned physics, math, history, and other academic material along the way.

Then came student-teaching.

As a junior I had spent one week observing in the school where I was going to do six weeks of student-teaching during my senior year. During that week I met my soon-to-be mentoring teacher. I also had the opportunity to meet another gentleman who was a substitute teacher at the school.

Returning to school as a senior I was soon headed to the small central New York village where I was to be learning the nuances of becoming a real teacher.

Meeting first with the principal, he informed me that the person I expected to be my guiding teacher had been fired the Friday before because he had just severely beat up an obnoxious student, causing the student to become unconscious.

His next words were reassuring, however, as the principal informed my new supervising teacher was the same person I had met the previous year.

Whew! My heart slowed down a bit and I was anxious to get going.

The principal had a meeting and couldn't take me to the classroom, but he said I knew where it was anyway, so off I went, ready to start being a teacher.

Turning the corner toward the science classroom I observed the substitute, now my supervising teacher, coming towards me with an armload of books. I was relieved to see him and was just getting ready for some morning greetings.

As he handed me the pile of books, his words caught me totally off-guard.

"Hello. Look, you were here last year. You know where the room is. Go get them started. I'm going to the faculty room for a cup of coffee."

Welcome to student-teaching!

The next six weeks were not what I had expected. My "supervisor" would show up in the classroom once or twice a day, sit in the back and take notes. His notes to me were always things such as "Never smile before Christmas, be like a drill-sergeant, they speak only when you acknowledge their raised hand."

His attitude towards teaching and classroom discipline were totally contrary to mine, and the few discussions about teaching we had ended with me defending my philosophy of treating kids as being closer to being an adult that kid... which they are!

My official time of student-teaching ended at the six-week mark, but the problems weren't over yet. My supervisor gave me a grade of C+ (which I'm sure was gracious in his eyes) and, after noting the grade and analyzing my scantily done notebook of the experience, my college professor who was also Head of the Education Department gave me a grade of B- for the experience.

In meeting with her, I tried to explain why my notebook didn't include any notes on my supervising teacher's lesson or why I didn't follow the protocol of writing formal lesson plans for each class.

After listening to my story explaining the amount of time spent in mentally organizing my thoughts and deciding how to teach each lesson, much to her credit, the professor gave me an A for a rather unique student-teaching experience.

From these events I walked into my teaching career with two crucial and continuing lessons. First, when things don't go as expected, simply adjust your original plans and push on to the finish. Second, when you have been wronged it's perfectly acceptable to confront those in charge with well-thought-out alternatives, especially if you can support your opinion with facts.

A Roommate

My junior year I started rooming with a person I met only because he was dating a girl from the same town of fifty-nine people I was from.

But what a roommate!

I felt comfortable immediately around him, mainly because he accepted me just as I was. I felt his acceptance was genuine with no hidden agenda or pretense.

He was demonstrably smarter than me, yet somehow our thought process worked well together. From spontaneous practical jokes to deep philosophical discussions, we agreed often and yet could disagree comfortably and without rancor.

An Engagement

And then there was this beautiful girl to whom I was amazingly attracted.

In our dining hall there were round tables of six or eight people. She and her girl buddies would sit together, and the first task I performed was trying to find their location. Walking by the table, hopefully seeing an empty chair, I would casually motion if one of them was free.

She was a freshman, and I was a junior who had previously vowed never to date a freshman. Shortening a long story, we were engaged and subsequently married during my second year teaching and her senior year of college.

I know without a doubt her love, encouragement and shared passion about teaching enabled my first two years of teaching to be a success.

Those two people, the first showing how to be confident in solid friendship and then second illustrating the staying-power of a committed love relationship, can give solidarity, strength and meaning to life.

John Hitchcock

Chap. 2 - Preparation Gives Freedom for Projects

*"You don't learn to walk by following rules.
You learn by doing, and by falling over."*

— Richard Branson

Now let's look at how a lifetime of preparation led to a career filled with enjoyment.

As described in the introduction, those events I describe represent fundamental concepts leading to a career in which the positive happenings far outweighed the negative parts of teaching.

Almost all the things described below were spontaneous and simply happened. No pre-planning or well-thought-out project or absurdities.

Such spontaneity amplifies the fact we need to retain or regain the freedom to be individuals as we enter the teaching profession.

The risk of being a radically creative individual is dangerous in some schools. You need to be comfortable with confronting colleagues or principals as you add to or appropriately modify curriculum. They will not always understand or be accepting, but it's okay.

I will admit class size plays a role in this concept. It is easier to allow individual learning in a class of twenty than if you must deal with forty or more students in a class situation.

Some important issues need to be mentioned.

- You must loosen up on the textbook. Use it, don't be chained to it.
- Don't fear Standardized Tests. Kids are smarter than we give them credit for.
- Expect a few "raised eyebrows" as you try adventuresome ideas. Not everybody will get it.

For the most part, I will present each of the following happenings in the way I taught. With few exceptions I never tried to explain the "moral of the story." I purposely allowed the students to develop what the event meant for themselves. Then as we discussed each concept in class students could begin to see the meaning of the project or event in the bigger picture of the subject and, more importantly, see how it could affect their lives.

Just a reminder, what follows are for the most part science oriented, mainly physics and chemistry.

You should look for the governing principle of each activity and make the application of how you could use the same concept in your teaching, whether it's art, English or mathematics.

To fully grasp the significance of projects and events I describe you must understand most were done prior to smartphones and Google searches. Not only that, but many of the project were initiated by students.

So read the following with an open mind. I don't expect you to agree with all my thoughts, but I do hope you can take some of the principles stated and include them in your teaching.

Unleash your creativity and gain freedom in the challenges of teaching.

It didn't take long.

I was almost one full year into teaching when it happened.

Three young gentlemen in my physics class came one day holding the magazine *Scientific American*. I was interested as they showed me a DIY article about a Carbon Dioxide LASER found in the section called *The Amateur Scientist*.

Their enthusiasm was fueled by the article because it gave almost step-by-step directions on building the laser. They were literally begging me to let them try building the CO_2 laser and entering it in the Rochester Area District Science Fair.

I was rather hesitant at first, being only a first-year teacher and still spreading my wings of independence. Their arguments were strongly supported, and I couldn't find any way to refute their request other than "it's not in the curriculum."

Soon I relented, told them about safety protocol, approved their request to use lab time and told them it would be necessary to give the class daily updates on progress being made.

Two months later the project was completed, the class had been well informed about Lasers and how to make one.

The took it to the fair…

…and quickly were disqualified from the Science Fair because unknowledgeable judges thought any Laser was unsafe.

Looking at the positive, those students learned about Lasers, had the opportunity to share their knowledge with others and, perhaps most importantly, deal with the disappointment of others who didn't understand the topic.

Similar, but different.

After two years and my wife's graduation, we moved to another school. It was in a small college town but surrounded by many active dairy farms.

Once again, I was approached by a group of boys, two college professor's kid and one farm kid. They were amazing students who had shown an interest in science from day one.

They also came with an open book in hand pointing to a picture of beta particles being deflected by a magnetic field. Their request was like the Laser Guys.

"Can we do this experiment?" they asked.

Same response from me. "It's going to be hard. It will require lots of work after school, you will need to learn new things on your own and you must give a full illustrative report to the entire class."

Even I underestimated "extra learning" required, but after using the school's beta source, vintage World War II powerful magnet, learning photographic darkroom techniques and many do-overs, they emerged victorious with several printed photos of "Bent Betas," which they named their project.

Their report to the class was interesting, even exciting.

"The Winner Is..."

We were discussing distance-time relationships in physics and the changes associated with friction and the acceleration of the object.

The question from one student was, "How far do you think you could roll a bowling ball?" resulted in many interesting and somewhat humorous comments from the class.

"You would need an infinitely wide lane."

"Depends on how fast the ball was started."

"Boys could roll the ball further than girls."
And finally, the question that excited the class.
"Can we do an experiment and go try it?"
The response was immediate.
"Yeah, let's go bowling!" was the consensus of the class.
I responded in a way that quieted the class for a moment.
"Ok, we can go. But someone must come tomorrow with a well-defined and planned experiment illustrating how we can gather and graph the needed data and the hypothesized results. The math must be shown along with appropriate graphing." Was my response.

Calmness for only a moment was followed by several students quietly shouting, "Go, Jake, Go!" as they urged the "math and tech nerd" in the class to develop the experiment and math.

Jake did not disappoint. The next day he proudly and correctly explained the process and how to analyze the results to the class.

Now the ball was in my hands.

Jake, another student, and I visited the bowling alley. As we explained the project to the manager his interest increased. Finally agreeing we could bring the class before the alley opened, he also offered free shoes for the entire class.

The appointed time arrived, and we donned the rent free shoes, found appropriate weight bowling balls and began the experiment. Using the lane at the end of the alleys where a walkway went the entire distance, we placed two students at two-meter distances with stop watches.

Each student rolled two balls, while others wrote down the data as we progressed.

We finally had all the data needed to analyze the problem. Taking the information back to class, the next assignment involved the students calculating, graphing, and displaying the data in tabular form.

The results were astonishing, far from the results we expected.

How far could you roll a bowling ball? Hmmmm…

Have some fun! Go try it. And you now have good apps, like Phyphox, which turns your smartphone into a great data gathering instrument.

By the way, the students had no problem convincing me while we were at the bowling alley to hold the First Annual Physics Bowling Tournament. The only condition I made was that the winner would be the student whose score was closest to the mean.

Sometimes It's Just One

Science Fairs are an opportunity for individuals to shine. Well, that is if you don't count the parent "helper."

This unique student certainly didn't need any help. In fact, it's likely his father could not have helped him.

The project was simple to understand. It had a large speaker (a woofer) on one end of a large diameter PVC pipe. The other end of the pipe had a rubber membrane stretched over it.

The project was an analysis of the frequency response over a range of frequencies (I think) and the display of Lissajous Figures on the membrane. Using an oscilloscope and other measuring instruments a relationship can be established between voltage, current, and frequency.

This data was then compared to the factory compiled charts as a reference.

Ah, ha. An interesting thing occurred.

The student came to school with data showing the factory chart was incorrect. After calling the company and tracing down someone who could understand the data it was verified the student was correct.

Frankly, I have never seen a student project more thoroughly done or presented.

The Science Fair soon occurred on a nearby college campus, judges to be college students, and the arbitrator of any difference to be the science chairman.

After a very nice dinner provided by the college, the awards program began.

As grade-levels were recognized, finally the senior awards were being given. We waited... and waited...and finally the Best of Show was being presented.

What? No mention at all! How could that be?

Too late to take action that night, I wrote a letter of inquiry as to why nothing was awarded the student.

"Well, first his explanation was so complex the college students judging (biology and math majors) were not able to follow it. Then we all agreed the math was so complex it must have been done by, at least, a college graduate or above."

Trying to be civil, I proceeded to inform the science chairman there had been no help and the student had done the math at school while I was there.

Lessons learned, and life goes on!

Galileo had no such problems!

Galileo performed his famous experiment by allegedly dropping cannon and musket balls from the Leaning Tower of Pisa. I've always had physics students interested in trying to repeat famous experiments, and the trend continued.

A group of physics students weren't quite as famous, and the results not nearly as accurate, but the reason was vivid. The experimental error was easily explained.

We didn't have a tipping tower to drop from, nor did we have cannon balls. We did have a three-story school, an old bowling ball and sufficient golf balls to repeat the experiment.

Let me describe the experiment a little bit, then let your imagination envision the result.

Half the group were on the ground with stopwatches. We had previously measured the height of the building. The remining students went to the roof with the balls to drop. The bowling ball was to be the first ball to be timed.

Full safety procedures were followed by not leaning unsafely over the roof line, the bowling ball held over the edge by a strong student. The countdown started by a student on the ground.

10-9-8-7-6-5-4-3-2-1-release...CRASH... OH, NO! What was that?

Let me tell you one thing. Don't ever try and repeat this experiment on a very hot June day from the roof of a building with crank-out windows fully extended directly in the path of a falling bowling ball!

Sit, Think, Write.

The day was splendid.

Not a drop of rain, sunlight flooded everything, just perfect.

The perfect day and the opportunity for trying a unique assignment.

I met the students at the classroom door and told them to take their books in, leave them on their desks and bring only their pen and notebook.

"We all are going out to the brook behind the school. We will walk up the brook, and as I indicate, one of you will stop at that point. We will continue until you are out of sight and another student will be left. This will continue until we are spread out along the brook, unable to see another person.

After thirty-minutes, I will come back down the brook and we will return to class.

You will take only your notebook and a pen.

Your assignment is very easy.

Sit, Think, Write." I gave the assignment.

Words came quickly. "What are we to write?"

I repeated, "Sit, Think, Write."

After several attempts to acquire more specific information, the students knew I wasn't going to change the wording of the assignment.

Making the trek up the book along a well-established trail was easy. The brook gave us a variety of ripples and smooth surfaced pools and plenty of woods in between.

I sensed a degree of uneasiness in some students, others gave body language that they were going to enjoy this assignment.

Thirty-minutes passed, and the gathering of students began.

Back in the classroom, I asked students to remove the page on which they had written and put their name somewhere on the paper. They were to indicate if I had permission to share what they wrote with the class or if they did not want me to share.

Reading or simply observing the students' efforts brought all kinds of emotions.

Some wrote only science related observations.

One student equated the brook to life, always flowing on.

Another wrote a short-story from the perspective of a trout he was observing.

The true artist in the class made a beautiful ink drawing of a rock and the swirling water around it.

The variety of responses amazed me, and it was rewarding to see the results of this assignment not found in the questions at the end of the chapter.

We buried Newton's Third Law.

Newton's Third Law is simple.

For every action there is an equal, but
opposite, reaction.

It's simple, but students often forget the word "every" in the law. Some actions seem like there must be a larger force at play. For instance, I asked a question on a quiz referring to a tug-of-war in the previous day's Senior Fun Day. The girls in the senior class won by working as a team and pulling the boys into the mud between them.

The question was simple: "Which team exerted the larger force in the tug-of-war?"

Must have been a bad day for learning because every kid in the class said, "The girls exerted the most force because they pulled the boys into the mud."

I couldn't resist the plan that flitted into my mind.

"You play the trumpet, don't you Tom? Can you play taps? Please bring your trumpet tomorrow. Don't tell anyone." Was the question I asked a student as he left the class.

That afternoon I borrowed a Starter's Pistol from the athletic department, the kind that fires a second shot if the first one fails, and a shovel from the maintenance department.

The next day came, and it was perfect. Overcast, very slight rain drizzle, appropriately moody.

When the class arrived, I was in a somber mood.

"Please remain quiet. Leave your books here. Follow me. Keep totally quiet. No one talk. This is a serious moment." were my very firm, but quiet, words.

Carrying the shovel, the starter's pistol, and quizzes from the day before, we started a silent walk down the hall, two flights of stairs, out the door into the light rain and out behind the gym where there were piles of fresh dirt.

Motioning the students to form a semi-circle around me I stood on the pile of dirt and began speaking.

"Ladies and Gentlemen, this is a very solemn occasion. "Newton's Third Law died yesterday. We killed it. Not one of you who could have helped it survive succeeded. Apparently, it has ceased to exist."

After my eulogy to the 3rd Law, I dug a hole in the mound of dirt, placed the quiz papers in it, covered them over with dirt, motioned Tom to play taps, and when he finished, fired the starter's pistol twice, to signify the two remaining laws.

The mood loosened, and we went back into the building to do physics.

Gift not appreciated.

"He didn't appreciate it. Just looked once at the spot on the wall, then went back to work. He's no fun!"

Those were the words of a group of students who wanted to deliver a Laser Beam to the principal by shining it down the hall, around two corners, and then into his office.

The procedure took almost an entire period, working with various mirrors, lenses, and a laser.

The students' excitement was quickly dashed and the opportunity for a principal to build his relationship with them also put on hold.

Immediately after class the principal stood at my classroom door.

"Mr. Hitchcock, was that a serious lab? What did the students learn?" were his angry questions when he arrived at my door immediately after class was over.

"Well, let's see. They could explain that LASER is an acronym meaning Light Amplification by Stimulated Emission of Radiation, learned the beam was there because of coherent light from the atoms being stimulated, that it's divergence could be corrected by proper use of converging lenses, front surface mirrors were needed to keep interference from happening, that dust raised by students walking by caused significant diffusion of the beam, but that the dust also caused the Tyndall effect enabling the beam to be seen. Other than that, I guess not much." My sarcasm was hard to hide, and to this day I wish I had been gentler, but he got the message.

I hate acronyms.

There is likely an acronym for saying that one subject can be related to another and be totally relevant. I haven't really looked, but I do believe that is a fact.

For instance, physics is related to art, music, math (of course), history, English. Duhhh…

One assignment for physics was to go into the hall where the art classes had their annual art projects displayed. Students were to observe the art through various color filters and report on the results.

The follow-up to that was an assignment where students created an art project which illustrated an obvious physical law. Then they were to write a short, short story or poem illustrating the concept or an analogy regarding it.

For instance, one student's photograph was of a bridge and its reflection in a very smooth and picturesque river.

In his written response he wrote a conversation between the bridge and its optical reflection as they discussed the technical formation of the reflection.

Continuing on in that fashion, the bridge-reflection continued discussing the dual nature of light (i.e. light has both particle and wave characteristics). He followed that by having the two illustrating the dual nature of man as sinful vs. God-like.

Another project which combined physics, technical writing and the head of maintenance with Science, Technology, Engineering and Math (hmmm... that's an acronym, I think...) was the building and observation of a Cavendish Balance.

For the non-physics people, a Cavendish Balance is a device showing how different masses attract each other and being able to show it visually and analyze it mathematically and graphically.

The writing portion was to include the submission of an article to a technical physics teacher magazine for publication.

Discovering many unexpected problems (i.e. static electricity, wind currents, large masses, etc.) the maintenance guy (thankfully a good friend), deep in the depths of his shop beneath the building, trial and error, multiple rewrites, the project was completed.

To this day I wonder just why and how the maintenance guy possessed over eight-hundred pounds of lead which we used while on the large butcher scale.

I considered it a compliment when the best writer in the class came to me and complained, "You knew, didn't you? If this was a regular school assignment it would have been good enough long ago."

John Hitchcock

Chap. 3: Student "Discipline"

*"To educate a man in mind and not in morals
is to educate a menace to society."*

Theodore Roosevelt

Somehow, I have been fortunate to not have to face many disciplinary problems in the teaching years.

Other than the ninth grade boy who I had to spank during my rookie year and the drunk student in the hall at 9:00 AM (not my student, just a random student) who tried to punch me, the disciplinary problems I've encountered are few and far between.

By the way, it's rather easy to neutralize a student who is so drunk he can hardly stand.

Student "Discipline"
Maybe the kid in seventh grade was right. "Ain't nobody smart from Dogtown."

For the life of me, trying to remember lists of rules regarding behavior is beyond me.

Early on, I simplified my list of things that make life good for all to one simple statement.

"Be Polite"

That's it. If we are polite to one another things just naturally fall into place. The classroom is calm yet retains a vibrancy and expectation of learning new things.

There have been a few times when "discipline" was required, and assertive action was required.

Delayed Discipline

Chemistry class had been interrupted several times by a student talking in a disturbing manner, "dropping" his books, clicking his pen, and you know the drill, don't you?

Affecting the mesmerizing lecture on chemistry (yeah, right.) I had motioned quietly to him a couple of times about his behavior.

I'd had it! Time for action.

I ignored his behavior until the class ended, but never mentioned a word of discipline to him.

The next day, however, I waited outside my classroom door. When he arrived, I gently blocked his entrance to the room.

Speaking very calmly, I told him, "Yesterday you were not polite to the class. Your actions interrupted those trying to learn. You no longer have the privilege of attending this class. I've made arrangement with the librarian for you to take this work there, do it quietly. Bring it to me later. We will discuss what you need to change to be allowed back to class."

Later in the day he came, and our discussion was fruitful and friendly. He returned to class, acted very politely, and we remained friends.

Sometimes you must ignore the bizarre.

Every school has "unique" students whose reputation precedes them.

Joel was no exception. His antics were almost legendary by the time he entered physics.

It was the first day of school. I was ready!

Or so I thought.

Most of the students were in the desk area of lab/classroom when Joel made his entrance.

He slowly walked in, stopped by the last lab table, crawled up onto the surface and assumed a cross-legged sitting position.

I admit, this was a perplexing situation. Mulling over several options, I decided to start by welcoming the students to physics, while totally ignoring the cross-legged, lab-table sitting student.

After the welcome, I went through the list of students, taking attendance and trying to learn names and faces.

When I came to Joel's name, I quickly decided to skip it, ignoring him totally, I continued to the end of the list.

Class resumed with no acknowledgement of Joel, even though several students questioned my ignoring of him.

The next day came. Same action. No acknowledgement.

He sat quietly, I taught totally ignoring his presence.

Third day, same.

But on the fourth day, things changed. He entered normally, walked to his empty seat, took out his notebook (still empty) and joined the class.

"Joel, welcome to class. We've missed you. I'm glad you are back." I said with genuine friendliness. And relief it worked.

Invading Their Turf

Football star, student council and friends with everybody, Ted was the envy of most.

Except he had bouts of not paying attention in class, even to the extent of distracting others.

This day was especially bad. Head nodding, little snores, even pencil falling from his grip.

Close to the end of class, I knew immediately how to react.

The class was immediately prior to lunch. Letting a few minutes pass to allow students to reach their tables, I plunged into action.

Going to the cafeteria, I located the table where Ted and his buddies ate. Approaching confidently, I had to ask another student to move down slightly.

Taking a seat directly opposite Ted, I indulged the entire table in small talk, mostly about football and being a role model leader.

The critical moment arrived, and I looked directly at Ted and said, "Speaking of leadership, do you think your inattention today exuded that?"

To his credit plus being in front of his buddies, he responded, "Absolutely not. I was wrong. I will make sure I stay awake."

The entire table and I then engaged in a conversation of practical actions in how to pay attention in courses that were not especially in their "interest playbook."

You need to give him a Detention

It was immediately after the last period of the day and about ten minutes before the "detention period" was to begin.

Four or five guys were standing around just chatting with me but acting a bit strange. They kept motioning to one guy to speak which seemed rather odd.

Finally, the gum he was chewing almost fell out of his mouth as he talked.

I couldn't help but notice and knowing the school rule against gum chewing, I simply reminded him of it and motioned toward the nearby waste basket.

"You're supposed to give him a detention," several of his friends immediately reminded me.

"You're right. I suppose it's mandatory. But you all seem to want him to get it. What's going on?" I questioned their apparent enthusiasm towards the coming detention.

Further asking uncovered the truth.

The other boys had received detentions earlier in the day and they, including the gum-chewer, wanted him to get one so they could all go together to detention.

I reluctantly wrote the detention, but as I told them, only because friendship takes precedence over paperwork.

Honestly, there may have been a few more, but that's the only one I remember giving in my career.

In fact, I would tell students early-on in the year, "I don't give detentions. Number one, that means your behavior is being created by force, and that isn't conducive to internally generating good actions. Second, that's one less piece of paperwork I need to do!"

Teaching Hippies... Real & Wannabe

The late sixties and early seventies were an interesting time to be a teacher. Political turmoil and social upheaval predominated society.

But in the realm of teaching, I admit to having a really good time.

Some were simply private times. For instance, there were a preponderance of bumper stickers. From "Save the Whales" to "No Nukes" were often seen, and likely represented the extent of the ability of the driver to explain his or her ability to defend their position.

My reaction to seeing those trite statements of craziness was to envision the bumper sticker "Nuke the Whales."

Sit Ins were a popular expression of social awareness, real or not, amongst hippies. Those methods eventually trickled down into high school, and my chemistry class was no exception.

Walking down the hall towards my classroom, I saw the entire class sitting on the floor, blocking my entrance. Not knowing how to do a real Sit In, the class moved aside just a bit to let me enter.

On the way through the seated students, I asked what they were protesting.

"We don't think we should have the test today. We are going to sit here until you agree." Was their response.

"OK. Well, enjoy protesting." I quietly said.

I walked to my desk, took out the gradebook and started writing, never acknowledging the protest just outside the door.

Finally, a student asked, "What are you going to do? What are you writing?"

"Oh, I noticed you're all here except Alice. She can take the test tomorrow. I'm giving those of you present today zeroes for the test. By the way, you've saved me lots of work. It's easy grading a test you never took."

As you might suspect, slowly the students entered the room and the test was given.

But the incident wasn't over.

After the test, I took time to congratulate the students that they made a path for me, they weren't loud and disruptive to other classes, and they allowed other students to pass by.

Then I continued, "But there is one more thing, and this is most important. I have to say, you weren't very committed to your goal. You gave up way to easy. You weren't willing to make your statement... and take the consequences. In the future make sure your cause is worth the risk. If your argument is strong, stick with it."

Chap. 4: People in My Life

I cannot even imagine where I would be today were it not for that handful of friends who have given me a heart full of joy. Let's face it, friends make life a lot more fun.

Charles R. Swindoll

I have been blessed...

That blessing always relates to the many people who have influenced my life and made it totally filled with enjoyment and stability.

First, I need to mention my parents. Their love, care, discipline, humor, two-hour mealtime discussions... so many things, so much wisdom.

Next, my wife and two-kids. I can't overstate the love and "living of life" joy they have given me. My wife as a partner in parenting our kids. My son and daughter putting up with my idiosyncrasies and failures. Love works!

The at-large family of unexplainable aunts and uncles coupled with wonderfully unpredictable cousins... life was always a new adventure.

But this is a book about school-related people, so let's go there and check out those folks.

Golf on each coast.

Top of the list are two foursomes in the world of golf; the East Coast Contingent of my brother-in-law who taught chemistry, a history teacher, a physical education teacher and myself. What great memories. Even playing during a hurricane in what we knew would be our last round together.

The West Coast Group teed off with the same kinds of teachers, ironically the history teacher being the same guy. Many unbelievably enjoyable times. Serious golf and serious humor made each round an adventure.

And great times discussing the ups and downs of our jobs.

Those men impacted my life immensely, and I remain indebted to them forever.

Love you guys!

Mischievous Mob of Creative Teachers

Both my wife and I were fortunate to be accepted into an interesting group of seven school personnel who became profound influencers in our lives.

From many school events shared (okay, so I was totally blue in the "Blue Man Group") to deep philosophical discussions about teaching and parenting, life was always being active.

One activity still is quite memorable.

Both the Superintendent and High School principals were attending a multi-day conference. While they were away, someone had the idea we should completely switch their offices.

Well, it only took a couple of hours, but we completely exchanged the two offices, even down to the placement of pictures on shelves and cups left on the desk.

When the principals returned, the high school principal thought it quite humorous.

The Superintendent, on the other hand, was quite irritated, thinking it was a senior class prank. His anger continued even for a few years after the prank.

"Okay, boss. I confess. We did it!"

One obedient lady.

The English teacher and I would sit at lunch and discuss what school should be like.

One day she entered the faculty room and placed a small advertisement in front of me.

It was advertising for a teaching position on the west coast while we were still in Central New York. A PhD degree was desired, and I didn't have one.

Not wanting to bother writing a letter (manual typewriters, you know) I called the headmaster in the west coast school.

Shortening the story considerably, a year later we were in the California school starting the last half of our careers.

Just think. Such a small thing. Cutting out an ad and bringing it to me. Small act – major consequences – all, I believe, God-directed.

Early principal and Times Long Gone.

Entering the large hallway area of the high school, I was privy to an unusual scene.

The principal of the school was behind a large football player. The principal was kicking the player right in the butt as he forced him down the hall towards the door and finally outside.

Turning around, the principal saw my bewildered look and gave a smile.

"Mr. Hitchcock, that's what I call being kicked out of school." He said with a gleam in his eye.

In that era of my career we laughed, the principal didn't go to jail, and the student learned a lesson… and laughed about it with us when he was allowed to return.

Two Bad Days in 56 Years!

Not all my encounters with principals were enjoyable, yet in retrospect, each of the negative dealings had some long-term positive effects… and some lingering bad effects.

The first bad encounter occurred when a principal of a Christian school came to me and said, "I don't think you are qualified to teach physics and chemistry, so next year I'm going to have you teach 8th grade science."

Caught totally off guard as the principal had never observed me teach, I logically asked on what he based his assessment.

His response was interesting, to say the least.

"I have no evidence. It's just my gut feeling." was his response.

Making a very long story short and experiencing the breaking of the principal's word, one year and two months later I had resigned and took a teaching job in a "gang-banger-central" public school near us.

The second encounter included both my wife and myself.

We had applied at a small Christian school so we could be closer to our daughter and her family.

After the first interview, we indicated we could not afford to live on the salary offered us.

First, they indicated they couldn't afford us. After some weeks they contacted us and said they had found a way we could be employed with the salary we needed.

We gladly accepted, taught a year in the school, experiencing a few "warning signs and red flags" along the way.

Within days of the end of school they informed us our services were no longer needed, based on rather untenable and absurd ideas.

We think we were used in a scam to make the school look better in the eyes of a WASC accreditation for the year. There is no proof, but the signs were there.

My wife's career ended there because it was right during the teacher layoffs nationwide.

Fortunately, two weeks before school began, I found a job back in public school. Actually, it was a God-provided job, and I taught the next ten years and then retired.

Good thing, too. If I was unemployed, I had already decided to stand in front of the school that had done the deed with a sign saying, "Will teach physics for food."

What's the good that came out of these two encounters?

Quite honestly (and sadly) one of the weaknesses of many small Christian schools is they do not have retirement plans. Nor do they sufficient salaries.

These encounters resulted in my reentering the public arena where I received enough of a retirement plan to make it possible to retire.

God's ways are quite unexplainable in human terms.

John Hitchcock

Chap. 5 - Principal Encounters

"The trouble with organizing a thing
is that pretty soon folks get to paying more attention
to the organization than to what they're organized for."

Laura Ingalls Wilder

Being evaluated by a principal creates stress for many teachers. For some odd reason, I have never felt nervous. In fact, I've always looked forward to seeing the principal walk through the door.

Very likely it's because of the Monday Miracle described earlier, but there has always been a bit of expectant humor I look forward to in their evaluation report.

Some examples of things principals have written are following.

"Mr. Hitchcock, don't you think it would be better to have two erasers at the blackboard rather than one?" was the astute observation by an insightful principal.

Another principal used a 1 to 10 style of evaluation.

On "Integrity of Teacher" he placed an 8. I couldn't resist asking him to explain where I showed lack of integrity twenty-percent of the time.

Failing to explain any action that showed lack of integrity, he agreed to raise it to a 9, saying "only Jesus gets a 10."

Never Give a Principal a Microphone.

Announcements are filled at times with unbelievable humor.

One principal loudly announced the following.

"Please disregard the following announcement."

Then gave the announcement!

I had to leave the classroom to have my own private laugh in the hall.

The next was from a person who talked in typical educational jargon.

There was an ice cream shop a short distance from the school where students frequently went right after school.

On hot days at the ice cream store the workers used window fans to blow outside air into the building for cooling.

The principal made the following announcement.

"It has come to our attention that students are pouring their purchased root-beer floats into the fans, creating a situation in the store which is highly undesirable. This action must cease and desist immediately."

The phrase "when the float hits the fan" immediately became the buzzword in the school.

Questions on a quiz can create a principal's criticism.

It just happened that on the semi-weekly quiz day, my principal popped into the classroom for an evaluation. The quiz was handed to physics students, and they started to write.

The class continued with me lecturing, students questioning, and the principal writing on a yellow legal pad in the back of the room.

The principal asked for our meeting regarding his evaluation to be that afternoon.

Going over his analysis of my lesson was predictable and perfunctory.

His last concern was not expressed, however, and I could sense a degree of uneasiness with what was coming.

He started his criticism. "You realize your room faces the street, and the image we portray to the community is important, don't you think?

Well, I noticed your shades were all in disorder and looked very unprofessional. Could you please take the time to make them neat and orderly?"

Unable to hide my chuckle, I handed him a copy of the quiz.

"Please look at question 5." I spoke.

5. The shades on the six windows represent a relationship between Ba-127 and time as we investigated in last week's lab. Explain that relationship.

I then explained how the shades were arranged in a half-life curve and represented the relationship indicated in the question.

Not being a physics major I had to explain to him how the graph showing the amount of Ba-127 remaining as a function of time allowed us to determine the Half-life of the substance.

His irritation at the non-conforming window shades did not diminish even as I tried explaining how the shades were arranged as a half-life curve of the Ba-137.

May Have Been Over the Edge.

Though I am a card-carrying introvert, there are times when the body is a bit ahead of the mind and the caution of an introvert vanishes.

Such was the case when I was observed for the very first time by a principal, who fortunately had a good sense of humor.

During my lesson he sat in the back of the room writing furiously on a large yellow legal pad. The pen was making scratching noise and the pages were flipping wildly as he took notes on my lesson.

By the way, yellow pads and violent writing must be genetic in principals.

The lesson ended, and as the kids were almost all exited, I got down on my hands and knees, crawled to the back of the room where he was finishing his written discourse.

Standing to my feet, and in an exhausted voice I said, "Wilbur, I don't know how you do it! As hard as I tried in my teaching, I just couldn't keep up with your writing!"

This Will Only Take Five Minutes a Day

At our weekly pre-school meeting the principal had explained a new task we were going to be required to do.

Trying to explain his rational for doing the task, he said, "I've tried it out, and will only take you five minutes a day."

As is often the case in which disturbing things are mandated, the faculty remained quite in the meeting, but quite vocal after the principal left.

I've never been one to be totally quiet but would rather go directly to the boss rather than complain where it doesn't make any difference.

So later that day, I visited the principal in his office.

I came with my coffee mug filled right to the rim of the cup. Balancing it carefully I made it safely to the principal's office. Placing the ready-to-overflow cup on his desk.

My defense for the teachers' position began.

"What do you want me to stop doing?' I asked, not expecting an answer.

"Around here I've heard you say, 'a teacher's cup is filled to the brim,' What do you suggest I not do?"

"Something must go if you keep adding five-minute tasks to the job. And if five minutes is added to an already full cup, see what happens." As I stuck my finger into the cup... which obviously splashed onto his desk.

To his credit, he didn't fire me, nor did he even defend his argument.

The only response was a logical one. "I see what you mean. I will rescind the thing I've asked you to do."

John Hitchcock

Chap. 6 - Faculty Room Frivolities

A little nonsense now and then

is relished by the wisest men.

~ Roald Dahl

Fore, on the couch.

The third "hole" of a short putting course my golfing buddy and I had constructed in the faculty room was the right end foot of the old couch. On this day, a teacher had her foot directly in line with my intended putt. As I putted, I said "Fore at the couch.

Too late, and the slowly moving putt bounced harmlessly off the side of her foot.

Later, the lady and I were at the coffee pot, getting ready for the next class.

As she poured the enabling brew, she muttered under her breath, "Mr. Hitchcock, some people never grow up."

I couldn't resist. "Mrs. Jones, I am not in charge of growing old. I AM in charge of growing up!"

Y2K threat

You may remember the ominous Y2K potential problem with computer devices.

In a moment of mental midgetry I wondered what would happen if the threat were extended to classroom keys.

In a matter of minutes, a very official sounding memo purportedly from the headmaster went into faculty mailboxes.

"All faculty, It has come to our attention that many of our classroom keys may not be compliant with the transition to the year 2000. We have configured the lock in the janitors closet across from room 105 as compliant. Try your keys in that lock, and if they DO NOT OPEN THE DOOR, immediately take your key to the teacher in 105. He has been designated the official coordinator to ensure all our keys are compliant with y2k."

I honestly didn't expect anyone to fall for the trick, but simply to see the humor in the note.

Well, things turned out differently… and six teachers tried the lock, keys wouldn't work, and delivered their keys to the designated teacher.

I had not informed him of the scam, but it was reported his first words were, "Hitchcock, what are you doing?"

Retinal Recognition

The headmaster in one school made a bad decision to install a wall mounted keypad in the faculty room designed to monitor the arrival time of faculty.

One Monday morning I entered the faculty room, walked over to the device and placed my eye very close to the red "on" light.

Simply sitting down with no comment, I awaited the expected questions.

"What are you doing?"

"Did that read your eyes?"

"Just like fingerprints, your retinal pattern is unique to only you." Was my only reply.

Well, the next day I heard via the rumor mill there were a few faculty who came to work, placed their eyes to the light... and, well, the rest is history.

John Hitchcock

Chap. 7: Lessons NOT From College

"Actually, all education is self-education. A teacher is only a guide, to point out the way, and no school, no matter how excellent, can give you education. What you receive is like the outlines in a child's coloring book. You must fill in the colors yourself."

– Louis L'Amour

Signs on the Board

I don't remember how it started, but there were moments in my career where I would post "possible signs" on the board.

They had no meaning, I thought, until students started to put responses on them.

One such example was the time I wrote "Today's Meeting of the American Apathists Society Has Been Canceled."

Upon entering, glancing at the sign, one student went immediately to the sign and wrote, "Who Cares!"

Sometimes a sign could illustrate a play on words.

In our town there was a steak house named Ground Round. I couldn't resist putting the message on the board, "Wednesday's Meeting of the Flat-Earth Society Will be Held at the Ground Round."

Famous Norwegian Scientist
I can't claim credit for creating this next bit of frivolity; I either read it somewhere or was told it by one of my many marginally-sane friends. I couldn't resist using it in school, however.

Once I started this, each year I looked with anticipation at the school calendar. When April 1 fell on a school day, my excitement grew.

Usually choosing the last period of the day, with about fifteen minutes left in the period, I started the addition to the lecture.

"Oh, I'm sorry. Tomorrow's quiz is going to cover some material not in the book. But it's easily learned.

So take notes on this and just spend a couple of minutes going over it and you will do well."

On the board the non-book lecture started. Taking whatever subject being studied, the lecture went in odd and unpredictable twists. For instance, one lecture involved the "Law of Catalytic Non-Reactivity" which needed a catalyst to be applied to a reaction which caused an intermediate reaction to occur preventing the original reaction from occurring.

I always made sure to include the statement, "This law was discovered by LOOF LIRPA, the only smart Norwegian scientist in existence."

Usually only one or two students got it right away, but a quick motion for their silence worked to keep the joke still happening.

The fun came the next day after the scam.

"I stayed up after midnight, and still can't figure it out."

"This law made no sense to me."

And the best reaction came as a phone call from a doctor-friend of mine, "I've been helping my daughter with this law and can't begin to follow the process."

We both laughed as he got it, even as he was explaining his grief in trying to understand.

Politically Incorrect

There is an inherent risk in doing chemistry or physics labs with high school students. In the safety of students, I was always stringent and rather demanding.

Some of the innocuous errors or mistakes they made shouted out their levity or "why did I do that?" responses.

It seemed logical to me to begin a process of giving some degree of notoriety to the students who created some lighter moments in class.

Thus began the "Dummy Goof of the Week" award, given to the student who did a mistake or action that illustrated the most not-well-thought-out event.

An example of such an award was the group of three girls (oh, all cheerleaders!) who heated some water in a beaker placed on a support with wire mesh immediately below the beaker.

The goof was that the beaker was a plastic beaker, and it seemed only natural to fasten the entire melted system to the bulletin board on which the award was given, giving the award in front of the class with a rather dramatic flair, followed by a standing ovation from the students.

Probably in this current era and the existence of "safe rooms," trigger words and cancel culture that would create a minor (ok, major) firestorm of anger. Thus, perhaps I'd have to take a step back and evaluate the wisdom of giving out the "Dummy Goof of the Week" award.

Then again, maybe not.

Flub Stubs

Every teacher makes mistakes, and I seemed to have distinct propensity for doing so, especially spelling. To the credit of my students, they were quick on the draw with corrections, always happy to get me.

Further thought let me to figure out a way to reward them, but also to make me be more careful.

Thus, the Flub Stub!

The Flub Stub was a small "certificate" with a cartoon character surrounded by several science related drawings. When I made a mistake and was noticed by a student (quietly and politely), that student received a Flub Stub.

What was the worth of a Flub Stub?

Well, a single Flub Stub earned excused the student from any homework assignment they chose.

Two Flub Stubs could be handed in for 100% on an unannounced quiz.

Or a student could hand in all Flub Stubs at the end of a marking period and have one point added to their average for each one.

Guess what happened... students paid close attention trying to catch me, and I paid closer attention to my spelling!

By the way, one student had a 99% average before Flub Stubs and went home with 105% on his report card!

Unexpected Lesson Prompts

There were times when the unexpected and unplanned proved unusually effective.

One such time occurred when I told the class, "Take out half a sheet of paper and put your name in the upper right corner."

That was the usual way I announced an unannounced quiz.

The students dutifully followed the directions.

The general procedure I often used in doing these quizzes was to explain a topic, then ask the question.

I started talking, but then observed the students were unusually locked into the words I was using.

Delaying the actual question, I kept "talking about" (I seldom *LECTURED*, rather just talked about) the topic. This process continued till class was over, and even involved some student interaction, which was also the norm.

Finally, my goal was accomplished, and I quit talking.

A student near the back asked a question. "Uhhh… what's the point of the half sheet of paper?"

"Oh, I'm sorry." I replied. "I've been doing a research project in educational learning styles and have discovered a half sheet of paper in front of students results in much better attention from the students. I have no idea why that works."

Another unique "lesson" occurred with James.

Picture a kid, six-feet-three, one-hundred-forty pounds, thick glasses, one gold front tooth, sprawled awkwardly in a chair in the middle of the room… and a smart guy!

Nothing had been assigned yet and my planned lesson was to introduce the main concept of Ohm's Law.

Starting with what I intended to be a rhetorical question, "What do you think will happen in an electrical circuit if we replace a 1.5 volt battery with a 9.0 volt battery."

"Wellll...let me see...if you switch out... batteries... with..." James started processing the question.

To condense almost the entire class period to a sentence, James continued thinking and talking until he had completely developed Ohm's Law (without the name), including resistivity, current concepts, potential difference and even the graphical representation of the relationships we could expect.

Both the class and I knew we were experiencing an unusual event, likely one we would never see again. When he finished the applause and shouts of encouragement were spontaneous, loud, and truly appreciative of what we had just experienced.

Use of Resources
On a quiz I tasked the physics class to determine how long it would take to hear the sound of a penny hitting the water when dropped down a well. Telling the class "You may use any resources available to you in order to find the answer."

A student called her brother, a college student taking physics, on the phone and he walked her through the problem.

She was the first one finished and handed in her paper. She was still on the phone, and it didn't take Sherlock Holmes to figure it out.

"Did you call your brother?" Whom I had as a student the year before.
She sheepishly said "Yes?" to which I responded, "That was a very clever use of resources uniquely available to you. Good job."

Solo Moments of Enjoyment
There exist moments of enjoyment that extend even into years. They last but are enjoyed only by you. And I'm okay with that.

Roget's Thesaurus was the starting point for one such moment that lasted my entire career.

Late in the night I was working on a chemistry term paper. Needing a technical term for a process, my mind just wasn't able to retrieve it. Thus, I turned to Roget. For you millennials and whatever the generation following you is called, Roget's Thesaurus was a book frequently used to find a synonym for a term. A reverse dictionary if you will.

Searching quite diligently for at least thirty seconds, I suddenly had a bright idea.

"I will invent a term." Was the plan infiltrating my mind.

It had to sound official but have no real meaning.

"Extraprataputilation" popped into my mind.

Kind of a long word to use on a manual typewriter, but the outcomes excited me, even those with negative connotations.

The day came when the papers were handed back by the professor.

B+!

The grade I was accustomed to in that class, and not a mention of a new or strange word. No underline, question mark or bad comment to indicate the anomaly.

Natural actions followed.

I used the word on other papers with the same null result. I even invented the feminine gender, "extraputeapratelate," along with different parts of speech.

You see what's coming, don't you?

It became parts of my teaching. Not much, just a spoken word in trying to explain something in chemistry, or a report for a principal.

Obviously there, but never noticed.

Well, once. By a student who noticed it during a lecture and to whom I gave a definition. "It's a word that can have any meaning within the context of the sentence," I explained.

Smiling knowingly, his response was, "I get it. And I'm gonna' use it."

Mixing Metaphors
Some solo-enjoyment moments are not quite solo but shared with those students who are really listening.

Mixed metaphors fit into this category.

I hate cliches with a passion! (Whoops! That's a cliché, isn't it?)

For instance, in some of my family/friend stories (see above) describing someone could be "He wasn't the sharpest knife in the drawer," might come out as "he wasn't the brightest card in the drawer."

Once again, the few who "got it" could be noticed just giving a slight chuckle or an inquisitive look.

Principals and Reports
There are times when solo-moments involve principals.

It is my private opinion the reason principals require so many reports is because they have a job with not much positive feedback for their performance. Thus, they ask for reports from Department Chairs and Vice Principals.

As a Science Department Chair, our principal required an extensive yearly report.

For the first couple of times I dutifully complied, listing things about budget, curriculum, discipline, new teacher mentoring, workshops... the list went on.

Interestingly, our meeting at the end of the year mentioned the report only in that he had received the report.

Voila! Never a comment from the boss.

The next year I dutifully typed a new Title Page. Nothing else. I made a copy of the previous year's report, stapled the new title page... and handed it in.

What do you know – never a comment from the boss!

This very efficient time-saving method continued for three years, and then I got a little more daring.

I didn't even replace the cover page. Just make a copy of the old one and hand it in again.

Yep! Same thing. No comment. No penalty.

Success.

Unplanned Classes

There are times when spontaneity happens unexpectedly.

I had posed a homework question in physics asking them to explain the acceleration of a rocket as a function of time and fuel load, then asked to sketch a graph of the changing speed of the rocket over that time interval.

Even before I spoke a word, a student made the statement, "I had no idea where to start on this problem."

Several hands shot into the air, begging to be heard.

Motioning towards a student near the back, he gave a wise-guy answer, "At the beginning, obviously."

Selecting another student by a simple extending my hand, she started explaining the process.

When her discourse ran into difficulty, another student said, "Can I explain it on the board?"

Nodding my head and with a grand hand-gesture, I motioned him to the front.

The entire class went like that. I never muttered a word. Only hand and arm motions coupled with looks of questioning or amazement. Even dismissing the class with an exaggerated motion towards the door.

A total class in mime! What a voice-saver!

Another time and school, but still the same unplanned action.

The chemistry class was seated, and I was on the opposite side of the room. I had gone there to get a fire extinguisher that had recently been recharged and placed on a lab table by the custodian.

Picking up the fire extinguisher, I cradled it in my left arm and started walking to the front where the fire extinguisher lived.

I had decided on my opening sentence for the class, and I started it while still walking holding the fire extinguisher.

"Bubba was his given name, and he lived up to it. But one day he brought to school two very common chemicals. We went out to the paved area behind the school. When those chemicals were mixed, after about a minute, the chemicals ignited. Flames were ten feet tall, the heat generated burned through the asphalt, making a significant hole."

As I was speaking, I noticed every eye was focused on me and the fire extinguisher. That focus continued and I figured I might as well take advantage.

I taught the entire class cradling the fire extinguisher in my arms.

To this day I wonder was the focus on me, the fire extinguisher or students wondering what the two household chemical were and if we were going to go burn a hole in the parking lot.

Whatever works.

Speaking of Fire Extinguishers

I usually demonstrate the concept of sublimation using a standard CO_2 fire extinguisher by shooting it off over the heads of the students in the room. The blast of white solid mist fills the air above them, but changes to a gas with no liquid phase in between as it settles down.

Quite an impressive demonstration.

As an aside, just a fringe benefit of being good friends with the maintenance guy who is interested in science and understands why you need the fire extinguisher recharged every year.

On this particular year, however, just as I was about ready to unload the fire extinguisher above the class, the Earth Science teacher walked in.

Too late to stop, I triggered the action and the CO_2 white spray spread out over the class. The result is impressive, kids are doing duck-and-cover spontaneously and emit some loud screams.

The Earth science teacher had never seen this and asked why it worked. I explained how it worked how it could be applied to the sublimation of snow in his class.

Several weeks passed and he reached the point where it was an appropriate demonstration.

"Hitch, ya gotta come see this!" The Earth science teacher as he burst into my room.

Quickly going across the hall into his room what I saw was almost unimaginable. A room full of student sitting perplexed and bewildered at their desks with white foam of the fire extinguisher dripping from them.

Point of information. Never do the demonstration with a solid foam fire extinguisher!

Early Epiphany Moments

One moment added years to my career!

My fourth year of teaching I experienced an exciting epiphany moment.

It was 4:00 PM, one hour after the end of school. I had stayed late grading the last set of labs. I was carrying the load of books under my arm for the work to do at home. My brain was frantically trying to remember what I might be leaving behind.

I was actually acting like a "real teacher."

Then came the moment.

On the second-floor landing I paused, looked out the window at the sunny June day, stood there a moment, simply contemplating what was happening.

"When I built barns during summer vacation, I never took a rafter home; and the barn got built! I can do the same thing on this job." were my increasingly radical thoughts.

I turned around, walked straight up to my room, placed the books on the front desk, and left the room a fully free man!

From that time, I seldom did schoolwork at home. I did develop long-term projects on my schedule and one that didn't affect my family. But the day-to-day drudgery stayed at school, based on the thought if I couldn't figure out a way to be more efficient then I wasn't a very wise worker.

One More Epiphany Moment

Frank was always an early arrival to first period chemistry on Monday. Our conversation was friendly, but often perfunctory.

This morning was different. He wanted to tell me about his weekend.

"Hey, Mr. H. Had a great weekend. Went to the mall and saw a new video game. It had great graphics. You would have loved it." Were his first words.

Then he continued.

"What did you do when you were my age? Life must have been pretty boring back then?" Was his question.

"Well, let me see. I grew up on a farm. Shoveled manure and other chores, went bowling, played golf, hunted, fished, went camping, climbed eleventh mountain, raised my own chickens, did amateur radio, skied on Gore Mountain, played board games, had neighborhood softball games with adults and kids, read a pile of Readers Digests, built forts… yeah, I guess it was boring." Was my answer, said as non-sarcastically as possible.

"Oh…, "was all he said, continuing to his seat at the back of the room.

Thinking more on that interaction, I began to see how hard it is to be a successful parent in today's culture. We had so many things to keep our interest level that it was never boring.

When "going to the mall" is the highlight of a kid's life, what a sad state of affairs.

Teachers are usually highly motivated people, taking their jobs seriously. Always grading papers, building lessons, filling out forms.

The present culture is experiencing many people leaving the profession early, simply quitting or making an exit plan.

Maybe more teachers should relax a bit. You can be motivated and expert at your job but can also learn to relax a bit.

Believe me, the job will still be there.

Teaching times are different now, what with the C,ovid Pandemic, cancel culture and gender issues, being "woke" and wondering which pronoun to use. It seems to me we could flip the switch and take on a more relaxed and enjoyable attitude, while still retaining the excellence we try and achieve by "always taking the job seriously."

Unplanned Randomness

Some things don't fit in any logical category but make perfect sense when looking back on how they contributed to the overall enjoyment I've experienced in teaching.

I don't remember ever thinking "I'm going to do or say this for…" any altruistic or profound reason.

They just kinda happened!

Let me share a few of them with you.

- Lunch-time discussions with a soccer coach about how we should teach our classes the way we coach our teams. Another topic was "does Christian music need words?"

- Entering the faculty room in a public school where several teachers were in the middle of a discussion about Darwinian Evolution. I simply asked the question, "How do you respond when a student asks you to explain why neither evolution nor creation don't align with the Scientific Method?" and the conversation shifted to "What I bought last night at Walmart.

- Lounging comfortable on the faculty room couch, eyes closed and looking very relaxed. A teacher comes in and asks, "Are you busy?" My reply was the truth. "Yes. I'm busy trying to formulate the very first sentence to begin my class."

- Dealing with a two-week absence from school, returning to the science office, seeing a foot-and-a-half pile of mail on my desk, picking it up and depositing it in the trash basket, and thinking, "If it's important, they'll write back."

- When a paper or lab report was assigned, I started answering the question "How long does it have to be?" with the statement, "Sufficiently long to accomplish the purpose you intend. If I say three pages, that's what I get, even if your paper needed five or only two."

- After finishing talking about a topic, the homework time (by the way, I almost always left time at the end of class to start the homework) came. I usually ended by talk with, "I'm done. You're not." Later a couple of students came and said, "We think that phrase would be perfect on your tombstone."

- As students were leaving class for the day, it suddenly seemed appropriate to say, "Enjoy being alive today." I suppose that happened because sometimes I had students who didn't seem to appreciate the fact that they were alive!

John Hitchcock

Chap. 8 – Introductory Chapters to *Revolutionary Education*

"The fact is that given the challenges we face, education doesn't need to be reformed — it needs to be transformed. The key to this transformation is not to standardize education, but to personalize it, to build achievement on discovering the individual talents of each child, to put students in an environment where they want to learn and where they can naturally discover their true passions."

— Ken Robinson

Not so random musings.

Earlier in this book I said that most of the typical schoolwork (grading papers, planning lessons, doing reports, etc.) never got taken home. I did mention some more philosophical musings occurred, usually very late at night.

During those late night times I reflected on some of the things, that in my mind, had a profound, yet not obvious, effect on learning.

They were not the typical issues. Not enough money, different groups of kids underperforming, too much hierarchy, and so on.

My thoughts went in a different direction.

What follows are some of those thoughts that played around in my mind during those late hours. They were previously written in a little book called *Revolutionary Education* and they are reproduced below as they appeared in the book.

Why I write this book

There are risks and costs to action.
But they are far less than the
Long range risks of comfortable inaction.

John F. Kennedy

The summer before my senior year of college I sold chickens and cut brush to buy my first car, a 1957 four-door Ford sedan. The odometer broke at 101,000 miles, the back doors would often stick closed and the rocker panels were more rust than metal.

Coming home from fishing one day I saw the vivid bright green of seemingly new rocker panels. My father was standing nearby and as I walked over to give the new panels an admiring kick, he said, "Careful. Don't do that. It's duct tape."

 The temporary fix of duct tape on rust didn't solve the underlying problem of deteriorated rocker panels. Nor can it solve the problems inherent in our education system.

The world of school.

Educational fixes often seem to offer the same method of solving inherent problems. More money, more technology, more training, more online classes, more acronyms; the list of new shiny objects hoping to fix foundational problems keeps growing. Each new thing a "duct tape" patch on a system with fundamental flaws.

These expensive, publisher-driven fixes focus on content with some well-intentioned attempts to address higher order aspects of learning. STEM, STEAM and Common Core attempt to provide a system of teaching/learning to assure success on standardized exams. As politics and publishers compete, the educational system begins to resemble a Band Aid-covered spectrum of acronyms.

And now the "woke" culture brings a new threat to the educational well-being of our students. If we don't align with their ideas regarding culture or fail to implement their false narrative curriculum, we are "canceled."

Life in the "Real World."

Actually, school and the real world are not different, yet we seem to treat life that way. What kids learn, or "not learn," in school affects who they are as people. Similarly, family life, "hanging out" with friends, job interactions, all merge into the dynamic we call life.

Problems and possibilities abound, and often we seem to always be reacting to both rather than being assertive in choosing the path of living that is best for us.

We don't need more duct-tape.

We need a radical revolutionary change in the foundational system of learning and living. This revolution doesn't need to be adversarial. It doesn't have to be a top-down implementation. In fact, if a revolution in learning and living is to be successful, it MUST be initiated and continued at the grassroots level of being alive.

Significant change takes time. It takes commitment. And courage. Most of all, a genuine revolution needs to be fueled by a clear vision of what can be! To come to fruition, strategic actions must be implemented to bring victory to the stated goals.

Since my rookie year, I have been perplexed why so many Christian teachers remained silent at school about their faith. Looking back, I suspect that attitude came from my Mother. Once she became a Christian in her early thirties, she took the Bible literally and talked openly and freely about Jesus in any situation.

I admit there are some legal limitations. We cannot promote a church, political affiliation or even a personal dogma. However, we can answer questions, make generic comments, and ask leading questions.

In the years that followed my initial wondering, I have reached the conclusion that education philosophy must be radically revised. In this book I shall propose a philosophy of education as follows.

1. Strong academics must be maintained.
2. Character development of students must occur.
3. The search for Truth must be ongoing.
4. The need for a worldview leading to a rewarding and serving life must exist.

Most Christian teachers are excellent at the first item, nudge a little bit into the second, but fail miserably at three and four.

In our present society of cancel culture, political correctness, racial distrust, virtue signaling, "safe rooms," and critical race theory it is even tougher to maintain a Christian voice.

We have become like cookie cutters. We line up as an array of entertainment consumers, wealth gatherers or "go with the flow" passengers in a constantly changing cultural universe. Our teaching is similar. We dare not deviate from the accepted norm, absorbing the same professional development workshops and giving the same "end of the chapter" questions.

"Doing your own thing" versus "Courageous Radical Excellence."

If you accept the fact that *the mind matters most* in everything we do, you will not consider yourself a victim. You will develop an intense desire to live with a radical excellence, defying the norm of living only for pleasure and self-indulgence.

When we think deeply and logically about how we are doing life, our outlook on living changes. We see others in a different light. We analyze our choices with logic and purpose.

We gain courage to live literally by the Bible, taking its instructions to heart.

In this book I am going to show how Christians do not have to counteract all the evils present in our society, but by addressing certain fundamental problems, often ignored, the gospel message can infiltrate the lives of our students.

Do not be misled. It will not be easy. Courage will be necessary. And wisdom.

As I read scripture, it has never been easy. That is, unless you call shipwrecks, stoning, beatings, jail, whippings and various other persecutions "easy."

We may not face those kinds of persecution...yet, but may have to deal with being canceled, called "hater," thought less of at work or deemed intellectually inferior. In fact, playing golf one day with a person who I thought was a friend, I mentioned I was a political conservative and my faith in Jesus was the most important thing in my life. His response was real and harsh.

"I always pictured you as intellectually stronger than that!" was his immediate and obviously strong thought.

Robert Frost's poem reflecting his love relationship with his wife is interestingly relevant to the world of living and learning.

WEST-RUNNING BROOK
Robert Frost

Fred, where is north?"
"North? North is there, my love.
The brook runs west."
"West-running Brook then call it."
(West-running Brook men call it to this day.)
"What does it think it's doing running west
when all the other country brooks flow east
to reach the ocean? It must be the brook
can trust itself to go by contraries
the way I can with you—and you with me—
Because we're—we're—I don't know what we are.
What are we?"
"Young or new?"
"We must be something.

Going against the normal flow is risky. Colleagues may be derisive or think you marginally sane. Bosses may be offended… or worse. Your children may rebel at first, but soon adulthood kicks in and your radical excellence becomes apparent and accepted.

As you make mind-determined decisions, you may lose "friends." Those friends you lose because you made higher order decisions will almost always be replaced. New friends, new ideas and new purpose will become a natural part of your being alive.

Priming the Pump.

On my backpacking adventures in the Adirondack Mountains of New York state, there were places where the only safe water came from an old-fashioned pump that needed priming. The sweaty, thirsty hiker had to take the jar of fresh water left by the previous person and pour it into the pump, creating the seal allowing the pump to bring fresh water to the surface.

Pouring the only water down the pump took a step of trust and confidence in bringing needed water to the hiker.

The purpose of this book is to prime our revolutionary learning and teaching pump. Let's take a leap of confidence and begin quietly creating a universal cultural revolution bringing a lifetime of passionate learning and purpose to our own lives and others.

On the day I turned fifty I wrote a simple, statement poem:

<u>The Hat</u>

When I get old
I don't want to be anything.
I just want to have a hat.
Not a plastic hat,
but one whose sweat-stained band
fits snugly in my furrowed brow.

I share that poem because it's important you know I am just a common guy. Just a normal, working, thinking and observing person.

A classroom career teaching physics and chemistry to teenagers could have made me jaded… maybe even frightened or pessimistic. But that is not the case.

One of my favorite authors, Harry Blamires, stated, "Idealists are the most tortured of all people."

I admit to being an idealist. Fortunately] also an optimist! Nor is it counter-intuitive to be those, and also a pragmatic realist.

From that perspective, I have been honored to work with many students and colleagues who represent the best of people. They have sparked my enthusiasm and created a strong base for my optimism.

Unfortunately, I have also encountered a growing number of parents, students and colleagues who possess several cultural characteristics and ideas having the potential to destroy the foundational nature of learning and living, even without inventing a new acronym. Most importantly, as we destroy the places where education occurs, we are ultimately destroying our country.

And let's be clear; education occurs at school, but also at home and work and just hanging out with friends.

We are traveling a dangerous path, but one that doesn't shout out its danger. In fact, it is a rather pleasurable path, one quite enjoyable and filled with open acceptance and extreme pleasure.

And that's why I am writing this book.

Life changes as we change.

Until November 22, 1963, I was a stereotypical first-year teacher; enthusiastic, passionate, motivated, inspired, questioning almost nothing. John Kennedy's assassination wasn't the defining moment in my global thinking about the decline of our country and educational system, but it was the moment that initiated my thinking beyond the immediate surroundings I lived happily within.

I began thinking beyond the daily lesson plan and started developing a deep-rooted mechanism of living-out my chosen worldview.

78

It took about twenty years for me to clearly understand the ultimate meaning and basis of my own beliefs. I finally could express what I considered the foundational principles radically affecting our daily lives, especially within the context of educating the young pe0ple of our country.

Simply stated, who we are and who we are becoming, entails two practical ideas.

First, *the mind matters most!* Everything we do or how we react is determined by our minds.

Second, *chosen decisions produce who we are today*, and decisions today determine our tomorrows. Without question the most important decision we make is "what do we do with Jesus?"

Do we follow Him? And if so, do we follow Him in ALL of our lives or is He relegated only to the "safe places" in our life?

I am more than a little hesitant to write this book.

We live in a politically correct, all-inclusive and morally relative society. Disagreement on almost any issue of importance gets one labeled a **hater** or simply dismissed as intellectually deficit. Many of the issues I shall address are politically incorrect and question the moral and ethical nature of much of our present culture.

I grew up in a family of independent thinkers, each one of us rather animated in our own way. We could debate any issue openly and with strong opinions. Powerful debates, but NEVER an accusation of being a hater or any hint of lessening respect.

Some of the ideas expressed in this book fly in the changing face of culture. I do not expect all my friends and family to agree with me. I hold real hope that those who believe differently will not allow disagreement on significant issues lead them to think my love for them is diminished in the least.

Holding those fears is real, but I feel a greater compulsion to express my thoughts openly and honestly.

Foundations of Failure.

It appears the general population is replete with criticism of the education system in our country. Recurring systemic complaints abound.

- "Graduation rates are way too low."
- "Young people have lost the ability to think critically or analytically."
- "Knowledge of our country or culture is seriously lacking."
- "Disrespect for those who disagree with us."
- "School curriculum is being *dumbed down*."

It's important to understand those criticisms are NOT causes; they are simply symptoms of broader aspects of the changing culture in which we live.

It is my opinion our cultural difficulties, including the nature of education, parenting and cultural interactions, arise because of the significant influence of seven radical changes in our corporate living.

- Evolution v. Intelligent Design
- Abortion v. Right to Life
- Gender Confusion v. Traditional Family
- Artificial Intelligence v. Personal Creativity
- Substance and Device Addiction v. Confident Living
- Political Correctness v. Open Dialogue
- Relativistic Thinking v. Absolute Truth

We shall address each of those foundational principles later in the book.

I must write.

What this book is NOT.

If you are expecting a data-driven, intensely researched document, this book is not for you.

If you are expecting a world-famous author, this book is not for you.

On the other hand, if you can accept a semi-radical, even controversial look at commonly accepted events in our lives and how they can be steps towards educational disaster... you will understand this book.

If you can accept something written by just a common guy, someone just like you... you will appreciate this book.

If you can accept a risky analysis of commonly accepted or enjoyable parts of our society... you may be enthused by this book.

If you can accept the idea that it is okay to educate students about the most important concepts of being alive, but need help in how to do it... this book may give you courage to do it.

By the way, there will be little "moral of the story" in this book. I will write basically the way I teach. My observations and examples will stand on their own. This is an experientially focused book. "Here's what I observe or think. The rest is up to you."

One more thing.

I am **not** writing this book to try and convert you to my way of thinking about the critical issues.

My challenge to you is simple; choose to have the courage to listen to ideas which might be counter to yours. Listen with respect, respond in your own mind without rancor or meaningless rhetoric.

Use your mind, build your arguments, and let's have a dialogue.

The same challenge exists for those of you who do agree with me. Leave the normal, intellectual dismissal of those you think are abandoning "traditional values." Listen without fear to ideas you find abhorrent. Turn your own rhetoric into reason.

Only as we come together with constructive dialogue will our educational system improve and thus improve the stability and focus of our nation.

Read on.

America, we have a problem.

In the 1995 movie, *Apollo 13*, Jim Lovell's character says, "Houston, we have a problem." This was in response to hearing a loud bang and several warning lights appearing on the console.

After analyzing the evidence, the ground engineers concocted a fix, making the problem manageable until the astronauts returned safely to earth.

For decades the loud crash of ill-prepared students has indicated *we have a problem* in American education. Multiple attempts have been tried to fix the situation, yet every election cycle the noise of the problem is addressed one more time.

It is my belief the problem continues because we are not focused on the root causes of the educational disaster.

Part 1 expands on two underlying causes of the foundational problems we face in genuinely educating the youth of our country.

1. Intrinsic and subtle activities and attitudes
2. Issues caused by a Cultural Crisis

An old, weather-beaten house cannot be rejuvenated by simply applying a new coat of paint. An appropriate primer needs to be used, thus enabling the new paint to cling to the old wood.

Similarly, until we understand the underlying principles and problems confronting teaching and learning in this century, our efforts will flake off and need a new acronym based program, giving at most, a temporary "feel good" approach to solving the problem.

I am calling for a CULTURAL REVOLUTION in education. We need to choose the courage to take risks, seek wisdom and embrace radical change.

Schools are Attacking Symptoms

We stigmatize mistakes. And we're now running national educational systems where mistakes are the worst thing you can make -- and the result is that we are educating people out of their creative capacities.
Sir Ken Robinson

In my experience as a teacher, early in the school year there is always the assessment and goal setting meeting. We are given statistical information that needs to be addressed during the next nine months.

- Our graduation rates are too low.
- Too many students were expelled or suspended.
- Math scores are still declining.
- The gap between minorities and white students grows.
- ...and the problems go on.

Then the lamenting and whining of teachers begins.

- Whatever happened to good parenting?
- It's those d*@&*#d smartphones fault.
- How can we teach if the District won't give enough money?
- We absolutely need smaller classes.
- If I didn't need a second job, I could teach better.
- How can you teach when kids don't give respect.

Eventually, the District or State decides to adopt the newest "shiny object" program to solve all these problems.

- "Johnny can't read" may have started it.
- Then came "No Child Left Behind."
- "Every Student Succeeds" soon followed.
- We need "Professional Learning Communities."
- Let's try doing "Social-Emotional-Learning."
- And of course, the "Common Core" national program.
- Currently it is the absurdity of "Critical Race Theory"

To achieve credibility, all the new programs must have the requisite acronym to make it sound important and memorable. Sometimes I suspect there is a federal or state division whose purpose is to create programs to go with the newly formed acronyms.

There is a major problem:
It isn't obvious, but almost all the recognizable problems inherent in the education process are the results of more fundamental failings of education itself and inherent problems in the broader culture of living. It isn't just the world of education feeling the brunt of these failings, but these difficulties have a profound effect on the broader scheme of culture.

There are some illnesses where a physician will treat the symptom only. This gives some relief but doesn't necessarily solve the real problem. It is my opinion we need to look more deeply into the root causes of problems in our school system and the negative components of everyday living.

The problem is compounded when "cancel culture" exists and any disagreement gets abolished from the electronic universe.

Maybe it's time to hunt for a new universe to exist in!

The Subtle Causes of a Quiet Chaos

John Wooden, the highly successful coach of UCLA basketball, said, *"Failure isn't fatal, but failure to change might be.* His words were within the context of basketball but resonate powerfully for both an individual life and the existence of a broader culture.

In the world of chaos mathematics there exists the phenomenon of the strange attractor, a point of infinitesimal magnitude towards which plotted functions tend to converge. Interestingly, in some of these functions, a point of radical divergence occurs, and the plotted function goes screaming off into a new abstract universe where the nature of the graph changes radically.

The historical educational pendulum has always behaved itself, oscillating around its own well-defined attractors. Fundamental academic ability, universally accepted social values, concepts of thinking, all eventually attracted the swinging pendulum back to an acceptable modicum of educational performance.

I fear this pendulum isn't coming back! I think we've reached the point of subtle, quiet chaos where the system is defining its own intrinsic principles and rules of education. As educators, we cling to a pendulum, but one whose path is no longer predictable and defined.

At times I picture educators in our own carnival of learning, standing at one of those game booths where obnoxious stuffed animals pop from various holes. We smack them back down with a wildly swung mallet, only to have another beast emerge from the next hole. In education we exist as symptom-smashers, blasting *can't read* animals down with our acronym labeled hammers only to have the *"can't do math"* animal emerge.

But in our current culture new animals emerge, now with faces of anger, even hatred. Hatred of our country, abolition of family values, systemic racism, critical race theory and all screaming agree or be canceled.

The simple fact is, we exist in an environment with high-potential kids, but with societally molded hearts. They come to our schools with unlimited potential... but polluted promises.

Have you ever noticed how disconcerting it is when someone else has the TV remote? Visual and mental chaos is created as they switch channels just as your mind is focusing in on your own interest.

That's how I've felt dealing with the students of our remote-control-generation. Just a momentary glimpse, then CLICK!... and a new event, a new deficiency appears.

"I hate that teacher" ....CLICK!
"This course is hard" ....CLICK!
"My job sucks" ....CLICK!
"We aren't in love now"........CLICK!
"This is boring".....................CLICK!

My fear is simple. Many of our students come to us with no solid conviction of the greater purposes of life. Even more ominous, the remote is in their hands. Compounding that fear, Dad and Mom keep supplying fresh batteries for the remote. In their quest to provide a good and safe life for their children, parents have acquiesced to being constant enablers.

"That assignment too hard? Okay, I'll call the teacher," they say.

"You missed the deadline? That's okay, I'm sure they'll still let you go." and once more the child is not given the opportunity to learn from the results of natural consequences.

Life is lived with the remote in hand. If an event or encounter isn't what I like, a simple push of the excuse button and on to the next more enjoyable event.

Booze, gangs, pre-marital sex and drugs are certainly difficulties and evils that need to be avoided by teens today. In my opinion, however, there are more insidious evils that need addressing. More insidious since they're quiet, appearing almost safe, yet corporately those evils join to produce a generation of students almost devoid of the most critical skills needed to live a productive and successful life.

Many of these radical things being imposed on us (even getting the right answer in math is "racist") are symptoms, and there are more fundamental things that cry out to be addressed.

The Flat Screen Generation

Students today are being raised by flat screens. TV, videos, computers, movies, video games, and cell phones create a concentrated culture of flat screens carrying messages requiring little thought or meditation. Almost everything kids watch today is at the shallowest, most emotional level of interaction. Car chases, dragons to slay, and videos with startling images enter the eyes, titillate the emotions, and quickly transition to the next intense image. Nowhere does the watcher have the time to relax, muse, ponder or repeat.

Should we wonder, then, why students struggle with critical thinking issues, panic when in-depth analysis is required, or shut down when readings contain polysyllabic words?

Flat screens rule. Not only do they rule, but they also consume. There was a day when little children woke up in the morning and did something. They played, they read, maybe even went and bugged mom and dad. Now, even young children slip quietly from their bed, find the remote and sit transfixed on the floor as the every-morning cartoons (or worse) enter their eyes and infiltrate their minds.

As kids consume a continuing diet of visual stimulation followed by emotional reaction, they can kiss thinking goodbye.

Ray Bradbury predicted it. In *Fahrenheit 451*, the elimination of books had essentially demolished thinking. The burning of books had essentially removed the concept of vision from the minds of people. Hope arose when Bradbury writes, "...Then he met a professor who told him of a future in which people could think...and Guy Montag suddenly realized what he had to do!"

We don't need to burn books to keep kids from reading. We don't even need to hide them. Just give the kid a TV-remote, iPod or video game player and the books go unread.

Francis Schaeffer warned us in *The Church at the End of the Twentieth Century* that "... men will end up owning only two values...personal peace and personal affluence." By personal peace he meant that men would hold to the concept of "let me do my own thing. Don't bug me." In Schaeffer's mind, personal affluence meant that men would have the economic ability to make entertainment and easy enjoyment very affordable.

The movie *Star Wars* launched an exciting new generation of graphics, and in so doing, may have generated a whole new way of absorbing information. One amazing special effect after another kept us on the edge of our seats, not thinking, but reacting. Movies started advertising the special effects, often more than plots or story lines.

So what's the big deal? What's intrinsically wrong with great action? What can be harmful about amazing car chases or explosions?

For starters, God wrote to us. He really did. And books require reading. I know that's a simple thought, but it's true. It isn't just God-words, either. Ideas are communicated by rather lengthy written discourse. For example, the philosophies and ideas of an American Revolution did not occur by a series of ten-second sound bites on the evening news but were transmitted by extensive publication and distribution of revolutionary pamphlets.

People read books and pamphlets... and the world was changed.

Having Learned the "Not"

Once upon a time, in a land that's gone forever, kids knew about responsibility and acted that way. Not all, of course, but most seemed to understand and accept the properness of appropriate behaviors in accountability, work ethic, and accepting consequences of actions.

Then society progressed. Mom started working outside the home, and the number of kids who acted responsibly shifted slightly. Many kids still acted properly, but an ever-increasing number began to act counter to what they knew to be right. Their behavior was frustrating, but because they knew the right way, that behavior was easily fixed.

Then came the nineties. Entertaining technology grew exponentially, single parent families became more common, radical-isms and political correctness were societally imposed, and comprehensive acceptance of a broadly defined diversity changed the way we looked at the idea of right and wrong.

Now in the twenty-first century we have students living lives counter to the positive characteristics that have been scripturally and historically based.

Students now come to school having learned how to be NOT responsible, NOT polite, etc. Profoundly more important than what's *not* taught is the inevitable learned lesson.

Let me illustrate with a basketball lesson.

One day on lunch duty I watched three of my basketball players doing some mild practicing in a one-on-one game on our outdoor court. When they finished, I called them over.

"Good job, gentlemen. Nice shooting practice." I said.

"Hey, thanks." they replied, pleased that I had noticed.

"By the way, you were very effective at practicing two things other than just shooting." I continued.

"Really. What's that?" they asked, surprisingly intrigued.

"Well, for one thing, you did a great job at practicing *not* blocking out your opponent when he shot. Furthermore, you also really perfected the technique of *not* following your shot." I said.

The point is simple. Our students come to us knowing how to use their "remotes" to make life choices easier, and they also come having learned their lessons well. Too bad it's the WRONG lesson. They have learned that NOT doing homework is okay, that NOT studying for a test the first time only leads to "credit recovery" systems, and almost any other NOT characteristic you can think of.

CRITICAL THINKING can be learned. That is a fact, and one that all teachers ascribe to. Considerable energy and effort is expended in classrooms trying to impart that skill into students. Trouble is, all those negative attributes contribute to a lessening ability of students being able to learn how to think critically. Unfortunately, there are also some subtle characteristics that can exist in teachers, administrators and the entire system that compound the difficulty of teaching critical thinking even further.

Approval by Acquiescence

Sometimes my neurological synapses operate slower than I would hope, so it's taken me a while to verbalize some of my thoughts about trash.

It all started with another of my many days on the ever-present lunch duty. I was on one side of the outdoor lunch area and observing the other teacher on duty as he was telling a table of ninth grade boys that their table trash was unacceptable. Having given the appropriate reprimand, the teacher turned and walked towards the gate. From my vantage point, I watched one of the boys deliberately and flauntingly flick a piece of garbage from the table to the concrete floor.

Old bones moved faster than I'd prefer, and momentarily the gentlemen and I were discussing the matter in a rather adversarial mode. The boys soon realized that they were, in fact, going to police the entire area, and as they worked, my thoughts slowly started crystallizing.

My next class after lunch was normally rather talkative before class began, and this day was no exception. Three or four mini conversations were occurring, and just as I began telling them to focus in on the thought for the day my mind went into Far Side cartoon mode. Suddenly it seemed to me that their words in this time of chatting became like pieces of trash emanating from their mouths and falling randomly to the floor. For some reason the following thought flashed through my mind.

By acquiescing to that which is unacceptable, we give tacit approval to that action. We give approval not only to those doing the unacceptable action, but an implied approval to those who only sit and watch. Approval is granted to their "sitting and watching" as much as it is to the unacceptable act.

By ignoring a wrong action, we are actually proactive in teaching a message, and the message is that corporate responsibility is not in the domain of individual activity. Thus, that which is individually unacceptable suddenly becomes acceptable in the greater, corporate sense. In the lunch area event, I'm confident that everyone would agree that it's wrong to throw their trash on the ground, yet by acquiescing to letting it happen, we have approved and taught that as an acceptable action.

Even more importantly, had I done nothing, and other students watched me do nothing, I would have taught the lesson it's okay to stand by and not address things that are wrong.

Law of Unintended Consequences

One of the standard safety practices when hiking or backpacking with a group is that the weakest hiker, the one who will lags behind, is always accompanied by a stronger, more experienced hiker. The weaker hiker is never left to fend alone at the back of the group. In accompanying the weaker hiker, however, the more experienced person must operate at a diminished level of skill to accompany the novice. In this case, the stronger hiker willingly stays at the back as a protective measure.

In most things we do there is an obvious distribution of skill and ability level, and the obvious observation in the backpacking world is that at some prior time the stronger hiker had been given the opportunity to risk... to venture ahead... unfettered by acquiescing to the norm. Someone, somehow had enthused the stronger to become just that, to learn the techniques and acquire the stamina to lead the pack. And now the stronger can help the weaker to become better.

In an ideal world, no one would ever be left behind. Life isn't ideal, however, and a normal distribution of skills and abilities naturally occurs. Someone is always the fastest, another the slowest. Some do calculus, others are hard-pressed to multiply double digit numbers.

The national intent to leave no child behind was well-intended, but statistically impossible to attain. We attempt that Herculean task by establishing curricular "*STANDARDS*" that can hopefully be achieved by everyone. Then we attempt to measure the successful attaining of those standards by using the oft worshiped and frequently cursed Standardized Test. (notice... said with appropriate awe)

For the sake of economy and speed, those standardized tests were almost totally multiple-choice questions. The Number 2 pencil and the Bubble Sheet have become the implements of war in the fight to achieve an acceptable level of academic performance. Not only are individuals measured by these exams, but also the performance levels of individual schools and teachers is directly tied to how well the students perform on these semi-sacred tests.

The commendable emphasis on establishing academic standards and measuring performance by standardized tests may have resulted in an unfortunate and insidious unintended consequence. Just as our students think at the flat-screen level, they analyze in the multiple-choice mode.

Kids are not stupid. They might not pass math or be able to write an interesting paragraph, but they sure do know how to take multiple-choice exams. The trouble is, their idea of "taking" a multiple-choice isn't what the testers envisioned. Students have learned how to do a cursory reading of the question, quickly eliminate two answers because they "look wrong," and then make a supposedly reasonable guess at the right answer.

For the past several years I have conducted an interesting exercise which substantiates that hypothesis. I select several questions that are multiple choice questions on standardized tests. These selected questions all have answers that are definitive or can be calculated precisely using the proper formulas. I then blacken in all the choices but leave them on the test so it's obvious that they are of the multiple choice variety. Sadly, most of the students react with, "We can't do these! The answers are all blocked out!" And unfortunately, they're right! Most of them are literally unable to perform at a passing rate on this type of doctored exam, even though the basic knowledge to do the questions is within their framework of learned material.

The importance of doing well on these exams can't be ignored. Graduation, acceptance into college, school evaluation and teacher performance are all evaluated based on often ill-prepared students taking curricular exams using faulty methods.

Life is decidedly not ideal.

Teachers are apt to fall into the mode of testing almost exclusively in a multiple-choice fashion. The extensive practice on weekly tests is thought to produce a comfort level for the students when they take the standardized exams. Another compelling factor encouraging multiple-choice testing is the efficiency of grading when class sizes approach the imponderable and unworkable in many schools.

Having lived with and experienced this syndrome as it developed through teaching in five different decades, I am led to the conclusion that an ironic result of creating artificial standards and testing incessantly with multiple-choice questions has inadvertently resulted in an overall lessening of critical thinking and analytical abilities. Ironically, emphasizing a multiple-choice style of testing ultimately results in a lessening of the very thinking and learning processes the system was intended to improve.

Internet Information Ignorance

Several years ago, some studies indicated that the amount of knowledge was doubling about every ten years. I suspect it might take less time in our present age of research and discovery. In fact, Peter Large of Information Anxiety says, "More information has been produced in the last 30 years than in the previous 5,000. About 1,000 books are published internationally every day, and the total of all printed knowledge doubles every eight years."

I do know that the amount of knowledge immediately available is vastly greater than the nostalgic era when many homes had at least one shelf of the living room bookcase filled with a neat arrangement of the encyclopedia just purchased from the door-to-door salesman.

To illustrate the preponderance of information, a few years ago, I gave a physics assignment in which the students were to choose a common technological device, investigate the primary physics principles on which the device depended, then write an analysis of how that device had influenced societal behavior, either positively or negatively. One student selected the flush toilet as her technological focus. After finishing her Internet research, she cited six separate sites devoted entirely to the operation of the flush toilet.

I'm going to suggest that you won't find six pages of information about toilets in any of the shelved encyclopedias.

This girl was a unique student, however. She actually read and analyzed the downloaded pages.

The norm of student Internet research is a bit different, as illustrated in the extreme by another student who wrote a social studies paper on the city of London, England.

His paper consisted of a Title Page and then twenty-six pages of downloaded and printed Internet information stapled together. When the teacher confronted him about this rather simplistic method of writing a research paper, the student defended his work by saying, "But I did the research. Look at that. I've got twenty-six pages of stuff. What more do you want?"

Obviously, that's the extreme, but it's more representative of the kind of research and analysis many students perform. They Google a topic, take a perfunctory glance at the first few hits, then copy and paste some marginally relevant paragraphs. Of course, the paper isn't complete until they paste in a few totally plagiarized and un-cited pictures or diagrams from the website.

Partly because of Approval by Acquiescence, Students have *learned the not* of a click-and-copy mode of research at the same shallow level of learning they use to take multiple choice examinations.

Avoiding Institutional Inertia

At some point in time, kids started going to a place called school. These places of learning strongly reflected the societal wishes of the historically traditional family. Times were simpler, and learning consisted of the mastery of a closely defined body of knowledge generally considered intrinsic in educated people.

Knowledge entwined with education often promotes activism in thinking. Certain aspects of this educated society then began to create a technologically based culture, the primary result of which was a rapid growth in leisure time. This richness of leisure time suffered the inevitable perversion into a selfish, *radical individualism* as described by Charles Colson in his book, *The Body*.

The decades continued and are summarized as follows.

1940 – 1959	"Yes, Sir. I understand, Sir."
1960 - 1970	"Peace, Man, peace."
1971 - 1982	"Listen, who really cares?"

1983 - 1989	"Hey, Dude, chill out"
1990 - 1999	"It's mine, Baby, it's mine!"
2000 - ?	"I'll text you when I get there."

Somewhere in this chronology, radical visionaries (actually, reactionaries brave enough to be vocal) began what we now call the Christian School Movement. Back to the academic basics, something called integration, short hair, classes started with prayer, and dress codes all became identifiable attributes of this exciting phenomenon.

First perceived as a non-Darwinian joke, the Christian School Movement slowly began forcing the public sector to consider change, at least publicly and politically. If you can't change the heart, at least you can put a cop in the corridor.

And finally, with the slow terror of a Poe-like pendulum, much of the Christian school movement is quietly acquiescing to the historical virus of mediocrity that has dulled the public sector. The safety of a dormant Christian status quo threatens to send this movement into the oblivion society reserves for the harmlessly eccentric.

No longer new enough to be interesting nor radical enough to be exciting, many Christian schools are illustrating what I believe to be a foundational law that governs many societal institutions. I call this phenomenon the Law of Institutional Inertia.

Radical Ideas acted on with enthusiastic energy give rise to visionary institutions. Those institutions then tend to produce rules and structure designed to protect their own existence, thus stifling the production of further creative thought and radical ideas which created them in the first place.

There is a corollary law that applies to individuals.

> *Creative individuals who dare act on their creativity reach levels of success which become comfortable and secure, thus lessening the likelihood of further creative action.*

The First Law of Motion as described by Isaac Newton discusses both the static and dynamic law of inertia. Both Institutional and Individual Inertia are static in nature. Creative ideas and enthusiastic energy allow an institution or person to reach a comfortable level of operation but staying at that level eventually and inevitably turns a groove into the proverbial rut. That *rutism* can be avoided by choosing to live by the third law of Dynamic Institutional or Individual Inertia.

> *The willingness to risk failure...or the perception of failure... by fostering and acting on creative ideas is the only way to produce dynamic inertia and to develop a continuing and expanding acquisition of Radical Excellence.*

To say it simply, be willing and anxious to enjoy the risk of becoming radically excellent.

Whether it's the Christian in a Christian school or one in the public school, our culture demands creative ideas that address the necessary ideas needed to live a rewarding and productive life.

If we really believe what we say about living a life focused on God-things we must develop creative ideas producing the dynamic inertia needed to achieve those results.

Not only do we need to develop the ideas; we need to act on them.

Culture in crisis

Hatred is something peculiar.
You will always find it strongest
and most violent where there is
the lowest degree of culture.

Johann Wolfgang von Goethe

DISCLAIMER: This chapter is most difficult, even scary, to write. It's scary because what I am about to discuss flies in the face of the chosen worldview of many people today. I suspect each of us has dealt with, or is currently dealing with one or more, of the issues that follow.

Cultural Crisis # 1 - Open dialogue and true tolerance.

Political correctness and an unwarranted meaning of the word tolerance have resulted in a world of college "safe rooms," perceived micro-aggression and a growing epidemic of teenage "anxiety."

Words have meaning, but that meaning may vary based on geographical location, history, and ethnicity. Hearing a trigger word for one person may induce a stress or emotion far-removed from the intent of the person saying the word.

Problems arise when the hearer of the word automatically assumes the user of the word intended it to be racist, sexist or critical. The user of the word then becomes a "Hater" and is considered intolerant.

Recently I observed a heated discussion between a transgender male and a straight male, both of whom had been good friends. The anger developed as the transgender male accused his former straight friend of being a Hater because the straight male was being "intolerant." By that, it appeared the transgender was equating disagreement with his chosen gender change as not being tolerant.

The straight male's response was totally correct.

"Look," he started. "The word *tolerant* means I can continue to accept you as my friend, even though I disagree with your worldview of gender identification. I do not hate you, even though I disagree with your viewpoint."

It is within that context I urge you to analyze the following ideas.

By the way, please understand. I do not write the following from a totally objective view. I have experienced directly or have had to deal with more than a couple of the ideas and concepts addressed.

Also, my intent in this book is not to produce an in-depth analysis of each of the following concepts. My goal is to simply propose these ideas contribute significantly to the current state of our culture.

Cultural Crisis #2: Darwin versus Design

Not long ago I walked into a faculty room lunch-time discussion about how best to teach Darwin's concept of natural selection to high school students. Ironically, one of my students had just asked an intriguing question.

I proceeded to ask the same question to my colleagues.

"How do you give a satisfactory answer to the fact that Darwinian Evolution does not align with the steps of the Scientific Method?"

The immediate response from one of the biology teachers at the table caught me off guard.

"I went to WalMart last night and got some great deals." was her *I-have-no-idea and I don't want to discuss it* response.

Sadly, most of the teaching of evolution comes only from the outdated textbooks often used. There is seldom any mention of modern evolutionary theories such as neutrality evolution or genome evolution. This lack of teaching more up-to-date theory is a significant lack of scientific integrity, even within the totality of evolutionary theory.

More importantly, the unwillingness of many educational institutions to even discuss alternate concepts is more unscientific. Genuine science discussion will explore all plausible options before reaching conclusions based on substantive and logical support.

For instance, from the simplistic nature of a paperclip to the operational complexity of an airplane, it is undeniably obvious they were *DESIGNED*! Someone or a group of people decided to make them… and then developed the design into a product.

The problem is, the simplest of living things is remarkably more complex than the most complex of human-developed technology. Looking at the amazing structure and function of single-cell flagella motors or complex brain cell operations should automatically prompt the question, "How did this happen?"

Such questions, though they seldom occur, are simply dismissed as "given enough time," any complex system can be produced by evolutionary systems. This bail-out response is given without rational mechanism or observable facts.

Why, then, do we fear discussing the dichotomy between Evolutionary Theory and Intelligent Design?

Interestingly, the teaching of evolution coupled with the exclusion of any alternate model fits completely with the "having learned the NOT" concept addressed earlier in this book. What is left out is never learned.

"What is Left Out" also teaches something

Furthermore, if we as humans are simply the current state of random molecular interactions, how can life possibly have purpose? If we are only a transitory stage, why should we worry about compassion, love, serving, poetry and morality? These are questions that desperately need to be addressed.

In my opinion the worst travesty of the evolutionary worldview is the lessening of the sanctity and worth of human life. And the worst result of that is the *Hidden Holocaust* resulting in the willful murder of millions of babies through abortion.

The continuous but subtle result of an evolutionary thesis is profound. If we as humans are a result of random molecular interactions, how is it possible for universal moral laws to exist?

Those who see abortion as a choice of ridding their body of simply cellular material have tried to redefine life as something fitting their convenience other than what life really is.

Ben Shapiro, a conservative talk-show host made an interesting point. He commented that if a single-cell that was living or once-living was found on Mars, headlines around the world would scream, "LIFE ON MARS." Yet the single cell human formed at conception is NOT considered life.

It's interesting how logic seems to vaporize when selfish motives conflict with fact.

Cultural Crisis #3: Addictions and Attitudes

A few years ago, my wife and I were visiting Yosemite National Park. Walking at the base of El Capitan we were overwhelmed and simultaneously inspired by the grandeur of this amazing feature.

About twenty-yards ahead, a young couple walked just a few feet in front of their young teen son. The animation and gestures of the couple reflected their own amazement.

Their son never once raised his eyes from the video game he was playing! His addiction to his device and game prevented any knowledge of the magnificence just thirty-yards to his right. To this day I regret not hastening my pace to be close enough to encourage the young man to simply look up!

Device addiction isn't limited to young teens. We have observed several instances of families in restaurants where each member of the family were focused on their device. Other times one person of a couple sits staring blindly into space as the other texts to someone else.

Other addictions still exist, as many have since recorded history.

- Drugs
- Alcohol
- Sex
- Pornography
- Social Media
- Mediocrity
- Apathy

The ultimate downside of any addiction is the mind-capture the addiction causes in the person. The addiction consumes their thoughts, thus diminishing creativity, analysis, thinking of productive ideas and even appreciation of puns or humor.

Cultural Crisis #4: Artificial Intelligence

Artificial Intelligence (AI) is exactly what the name says; computers and machines designed by people to take over tasks or procedures normally done by people. These tasks are often life-saving, work-reducing or simply enjoyment-creating events.

Take a look at just some of the items in our lives qualifying as AI.

- Directional Instructions by GPS apps
- ATM machines or total banking apps
- Is Siri smarter than the homeowner?
- Lifelike robots as friends
- Endless automated phone instructions
- Easy-pay apps at gas stations and stores
- Online courses that tutor and grade work
- Robot controlled medical diagnosis and treatment
- Transhumanism and immortality (look it up…)
- Automatic spelling and grammar checking
- Voice to text apps and text to voice
- The "smart home" and "smart appliances"
- Smart Cars

That list barely taps the surface of AI involvement in our lives. Try this: for one week; keep a list of every single time you use or encounter something qualifying as

Artificial Intelligence. Interestingly, the hardest part might prove to be recognizing the activity as AI. For instance, what about the traffic light that changes only when a vehicle is approaching from a given direction? Did you count that?

Please keep this in mind. Most things involving AI are legitimately classified as "good." They help us, they are beneficial individually and corporately.

The problem is quietly insidious. If our easy lives create a sense of dependence then when something unusual occurs, we may never have developed a sense of how to handle a difficult situation.

You see, one fact of an increasing dominance of Artificial Intelligence is *we no longer fix things.*

When I was about fourteen years old, our rotary dial phone stopped working. It made a quiet buzz, but the loud, attention getting ring was missing.

"Do you think you can fix it?" my mother asked with some degree of optimism in her question, likely because she had observed me building my amateur radio equipment. Living on a farm also contributed to the logic of repair since that's what farmers do... they fix things. Or at least they used to.

Using a Phillips screwdriver and my favorite needle-nose pliers I dismantled the device, adjusted a few screws and had the ring back again. Interestingly, I didn't have to spend twenty minutes selecting a new ringtone. What you had was what you got.

It's not that simple now.

If we can't fix a non-working electronic device by a software update or talking to the guy in India, we hope our two-year contract is up and we qualify for an upgrade. If that's the case, our life is stable again and we get on with texting, watching viral videos of cats, babies or the most recent "cop shoots kid" event.

Our old, hard-wired phones did only one thing; they made calls. They didn't tell us where we were, had no calculator or act as a camera or flashlight. They couldn't even hook up to Google... errrr... wait... Google hadn't been invented yet.

On the other hand, those old klunkers didn't spy on us, give out personal information to the bad guys or become an addictive EED. (Electronic Enjoyment Device)

The good, the bad and the ugly.

Whether being held Linus-blanket-like in our hands or hidden in the deep recesses of our car, smart devices have become the ubiquitous necessity of our age. As long as a cell tower is in electronic sight hikers no longer need to worry about moss on the northwest side of trees, travelers never have to meet interesting people who give verbal directions to the best diner in town or we never have to interpret body language or voice inflection as conversations are reduced to text-language acronyms.

Who really cares? Life is good, especially when Facebook allows us to share with all our electronic friends that we just went to Walmart and recognized the greeter as our next door neighbor. LOL!

Sometimes I wonder... maybe a good EMP would be a welcome event, forcing us to rekindle (pun intended) the skill of critical thinking.

And if you don't know what that last sentence means, there is always Google.

Cultural Crisis #5: Redefined Relationships

There was a time, not so long ago, when the concept of family meant one thing: a female mother, male father and boys or girls as kids. Of course, there were variations on that theme, but the implied norm was the traditional family.

Early in my teaching career the concept of a "melting pot" America meant the development of our country by the melding together of immigrants from many countries and customs.

The melting pot has become a cultural stew. In the latter part of my teaching career, the following list of terms could be used to describe the nature of various families in our schools.

The single most influential event resulting in massive change may have been World War II. Men went off to war and women went to work. It wasn't just that Mom was no longer at home raising kids. Now single women began choosing career over convention.

This transition is certainly not bad, but it did initiate a transition from tradition to a more independent and open life.

As life expectations and goals changed, those ideas and concepts long considered "normal" took on new meaning.

Twenty-first century living is now open and culturally accepting of a radical change in lifestyle.

Now, when students enter our classroom or show up on our socially distant screen, one or more of the following descriptors may be relevant.

Representative Terms of Family Groups

Nuclear family	Drug addicted	Homeless
Racially mixed	Alcoholic	Cult members
Gay	Working parents	Strict
Lesbian	Porn stars	Liberal
Divided	Enabling	Conservative
Divorced	Rich	Humanists
Abusive	Poor	Transgender
Illegals	Transients	Unemployed

Without question, these various groupings have always existed, and most importantly, co-existed without rancor and perceived hatred.

All that changed with the advent of identity culture and misuse of the word tolerance. At some point it became necessary to be known by a certain label. Not only known by that label, but others were expected to agree with the chosen lifestyle.

No longer was it possible to live harmoniously in a diverse community, but you were expected to agree with all others. Obviously there have always been those who aggressively disagreed with and treated others poorly. They were generally a minority and were opposed by people on both sides of any lifestyle.

This expected agreement with all lifestyles resulted in our next cultural crisis.

Cultural Crisis #6: The Death of Dialogue

In any context we should always be sensitive to how our words may affect others. Blatant disrespect or hurtful comments are never acceptable.

Problems arise when unwarranted and extreme perception interprets words as being disrespectful or demeaning even though the user of the word held neither of those attitudes. A lecturer describing an electrical engineer as "he" is not creating exclusivity nor is a textbook showing a picture of a woman nurse being stereotypical.

Over-reaction to another's words has created a subtle fear of speaking out on a subject. Who knows? The speaker might use a "politically incorrect" phrase that changes the intended dialogue to one of dissent over having offended the listener. The tendencies have thus become silence on one side or running off to a college-level "safe room" to cuddle a friendly Teddy Bear.

Whoops! Sorry. Teddy is likely sexist. Should have said "...to cuddle a *They* Bear."

This whole idea of political correctness has created a dynamic mix of conflicting attitudes and ideas.

Disagreement about ideas, philosophies or lifestyle choices do not make you a hater or intolerant. More importantly, disagreement does not prevent you from loving the one with whom you disagree. In fact, appropriately discussed disagreements help you become more insightful, analytical, maybe even creative.

Whether intended or not, political correctness has become a mechanism for defending weak ideas. If a person or group holds to an idea, philosophy or lifestyle which cannot be defended by logic or fact, one or more of the following occur.

- People or speakers with opposing views are shouted down
- Opposing views are ridiculed or laughed at derisively
- Protests by groups are held, preventing opposing events

- Those with opposing views are totally ignored or never reported on
- Derogatory terms like racist or bigot are rendered

Ironically, many of those who hold others to politically correct thinking have no problem with espousing openly contradictory statements or actions.

For instance, one state in which I taught openly said, "You are never to state your personal political view in the classroom." Then, in a mandatory workshop, teachers were informed it was now required to "mention specifically the gay lifestyle of selected scientists, poets, historians, etc."

Here is the real irony; to bring either of those issues up for public debate would have been considered unacceptable and adversarial.

For those willing to observe the society in which we live, the next crisis is obvious.

Cultural Crisis #7: Moral Relativism

"What's wrong with copying someone's homework? It doesn't hurt anybody." That sentence is heard on a regular basis by teachers who have uncovered blatant cheating.

One teacher discovered a supposedly original poem copied word for word from a famous author. The **mother's** words were astounding; "It's just a coincidence my daughter wrote those same words."

A student handed in an eighteen page paper with only the title page his original work. The remaining pages were literally copy and pasted from online websites. When being confronted, the student's response was, "But I did the research and found all that stuff."

It isn't only school where moral integrity is compromised. We all are likely familiar with politicians who solicit our votes by promising certain actions when elected. Once in office their votes are contrary to those promises to gain favor with other politicians or external interest groups.

Society is replete with telephone and Internet scams, lying salesmen, shoplifting and a plethora of other misleading or totally false circumstances.

Even in the most fundamental of all decisions, the choice of a life-directing worldview is rationalized by saying, "It doesn't matter what you believe as long as you are serious about it."

How did we get to this awful place?

The re-writers of American history would do well to actually read the Declaration of Independence.

"...When, in the course of human events, it becomes necessary for one people to dissolve the political bonds which have connected them with another, and to assume among the powers of the earth, the separate and equal station to which the laws of nature and of nature's God entitle them, a decent respect to the opinions of mankind requires that they should declare the causes which impel them to the separation.

We hold these truths to be self-evident, that all men are created equal, that they are endowed by their Creator with certain unalienable rights, that among these are life, liberty and the pursuit of happiness..."

I graduated from high school in 1959. That was the year the original lawsuit was filed to ban the following from public schools.

"Almighty God, we acknowledge our dependence on Thee, and we beg Thy blessings upon us, our parents, our teachers and our country."

We recited that prayer together immediately after saying the pledge to the American flag.

"I pledge allegiance to the Flag of the United States of America, and to the Republic for which it stands, one Nation under God, indivisible, with liberty and justice for all."

The important point of the preceding quotes isn't only the mention of a God-Creator, but also the inference a standard existed. Concepts of right and wrong do exist, regardless of those who promote the false narrative of revisionist history.

The problem, however, isn't just the continuing false narrative. The reality is that many in the general population have no comprehension of the significance of our historical documents and the principles on which they were founded. That fatal ignorance, in my opinion, is the systemic failure of our educational system.

I posit that moral relativism is the expected result of a combination of evolutionary thinking, political correctness, the attempt at philosophical inclusion and the misinterpretation of the concept of tolerance.

Parents know that what isn't taught almost always results in the opposite of the missing lesson. If a child is never taught about sharing the ultimate selfishness of "mine" becomes the acquired lesson.

Similarly, if public schools never really teach the character values illustrated in the Judeo-Christian tradition on which our nation is based, the only logical learned lesson is that moral relativism is the accepted worldview.

Absolute Truth exists. Just because you believe something deeply and sincerely doesn't make it true.

Here's the irony. Those who maintain there is no Absolute Truth want us to believe that their truth is absolute! If we say evolution is true... it is. If we say life doesn't happen until birth... it is.

Our Truth is based on an external source, the Bible and supported by historical events and observations of the universe. This fact drives our hearts and actions.

We need to hold firm to this.

And take action!

John Hitchcock

Chap. 9 – I'm Done. You're Not

Now I am retired. This time for real, or unless another part time position jumps into my life. It would have to be almost ideal as far as schedule or desire, but it's a possibility.

I admit to enjoying retirement. Being able to determine my own schedule with very few hard and fast obligations.

When I look back on my career I have been genuinely blessed. My students, principals, friends, events and the everyday environment joined together into a massively enjoyable time.

The spectrum of my career.

As I look at teaching now, I often wonder how I would fit in.

My career covered a broad spectrum of school experiences. Small public school, large public school, "gang banger" school, farm kids, city kids, combinations of students, Christian school, Independent Study school, homeschool oriented school… a potpourri of students and teachers.

Class size ranged from seven students to forty students in a room designed for twenty-eight. Laboratory facilities ranged from excellent to less than adequate.

I had to deal with the inconvenience of two building projects, including one with two shifts of teaching.

When I started teaching the teachers' unions did not exist. They then became prevalent and gradually became less involved with the benefit of teachers but more concerned with retaining their own power, both political and cultural.

Many of those things were inconvenient, but none of them were of such a nature to destroy the enjoyment of going to work each day.

What about now?

The teacher of today faces a more diverse and possibly enjoyment-killing job.

The list is rather unique. Gender identity issues, the "woke" culture, hiding things from parents, cancel culture, social media, bullying, school shootings, critical race theory, cross-dressers doing workshops, mandatory acknowledge of historical figure LGBTQ nature, racism, revisionist history, micro-aggression are all issues that potentially exist in your school.

The bizarre has become commonplace. In fact, political incorrectness looks quite mild compared to many of the issues prevalent in schools today.

The ongoing issues still exist. Disrespect of teachers, low pay, extra work, standardized tests, mandated curriculum, Peter-Principle Principals…some things never disappear.

Currently more teachers are expressing a total dissatisfaction with their job, retiring early or simply walking off the job. Several express the fact they wake each morning dreading the day ahead. Not only that, but the supply chain of college students also preparing to become teachers is lower than ever.

Would I have survived?

Honestly, I don't know. Never having to deal with much of what's the norm today I can't honestly answer that question.

I can hypothesize a bit, though.

First, I cannot begin to imagine being silent on many of those issues, either asking thoughtful questions or maybe even those questions which present a dilemma.

Second, in the last school I was in there were some transgender students. I found they were very responsive when I engaged them in conversation, even asking what about their bodies let to the decision to transition. The point is, when discussion is initiated with respect, people generally respond respectfully.

Some of the "woke culture" or white supremacy movement lend themselves to quiet humor. How in the world can math be considered racist?

I understand how those who try to make it so think, but there are flaws in the reasoning that need to be exposed.

My hope is that I would not be afraid to try and expose those flaws, even though it would likely not be cheerfully accepted.

However...

It's likely I would be fired!

How about you?

Maybe you are in a school that is still quite traditional and not subject to all the weird behaviors of the culture today.

Good for you, and I hope this book can be an encouragement and maybe even a help toward the enjoyment of your job.

If you teach in one of the more "progressive" (that name has always seemed like an oxymoron to me) schools, I understand your problem and can have some degree of empathy.

Here is my one word of encouragement.

Believe me, I pray for you. I pray for your patience, your perseverance and maybe most of all, your courage to stand strong.

To stand strong, and to find ways to fight against those things that are blatantly wrong.

As my nonagenarian Uncle Gord used to end his letters…

Fight the fight. Keep the faith.

About the Author

John never considered himself a revolutionary nor an activist; he was simply living and thinking in the way he had been taught.

- It was natural to look at any action and ask if there was a better way to accomplish it.
- To ask the question "why are we doing this?"
- Never issue a complaint without a solution.
- Always ask "is someone or some group being hurt by this?"
- Is this curriculum true… or false?
- Does the curriculum violate Scripture?
- Are there bigger issues at play?
- What factors influence my students? Good or bad?
- Does what I'm teaching represent True Truth of God?

And bosses… some of them thought of him as an irritant. They were offended if John questioned anything. Open dialogue was never on the table.

The Strategy Develops

By nature, John is an introvert. But not one who could stand by and be silent when something needed addressing or there was an opportunity to tell about Jesus.

- His quiet nature allowed hard things to be said without offense.
- He learned somethings were better said in an open meeting with faculty.
- Others should be to the boss privately.
- Some things should be done in writing.
- Not being the first to talk could be beneficial.
- Biblical truths could be expressed but without references.
- Some topics could be initiated by a question then expounded on later and individually.
- It was risky to deviate from the expected, but so worth it.
- Praying at the start of class for wisdom worked wonders. Silently in public school, verbally in Christian schools.

So, there you have it. A fifty-six year career teaching kids about life and how to live it well using physics and chemistry as the vehicle for the message.

And before "I'm Done, You're Not!" becomes his epitaph John hopes to be able to say he "enjoyed life by being alive."

Other Books by John Hitchcock

Paperbacks:

- Radical Excellence
- Play Smart Golf Today
- Common Sense Learning and Living

Ebooks:

- A+ Parenting
- Good Bogey – Bad Bogey
- Get a Grip – Join Life
- Live Better from the Inside Out

Journals:

- Bible Study Your Way
- Adirondack Adventure Journal
- Golf Score Journal
- Homeschool Lifetime Learning: Physics

Made in the USA
Monee, IL
24 August 2022

12378273R00069